THE PERSUASIVE

MARKETER

Key Focus on Mastering the Arts of Selling

Anything to Anybody

IOANNIS ANTYPAS

Absolute Author Publishing House

Absolute Author
Publishing House

Publisher: Absolute Author Publishing House
Author: Ioannis Antypas
Editor: Dr. Melissa Caudle
Cover Designer: Prudence Makhura

LIBRARY OF CONGRESS CATALOGING-IN-PUBLICATION DATA

Antypas, Ioannis
    The Persuasive Marketer/Ioannis Antypas

        p. cm.

ISBN: 978-1-951028-96-1

1. Business   2. Marketing   3. Finance

TABLE OF CONTENTS

SYNOPSIS

Marketing on the most basic is neither about the marketer nor the product to be marketed; it is always about the buyer -- your audience, your prospect. The concept of marketing focuses on understanding the vulnerability of your audience, their weakness, and providing the best solution to them. This means the success of your marketing comes from understanding your buyer, their problems, and giving them the best offer. Sometimes, selling is not the best thing to do to a new prospect; sometimes, it was only about understanding their pain and having to communicate with them in a tone that creates trust and hopes to them.

Not everyone wants to be sold to; however, they need a solution to their problem. With this book "The Persuasive Marketer," you will be opened to a new realm of marketing, where you can leverage on the weakness of your audience, not to exploit them, but to proffer solution them and generate sales on your side.

This book details the latest concept of marketing, the importance of communication, copywriting, lead generation, storytelling, the psychology of selling, and more, to improve your business, increase sales and improve your marketing skills.

Marketing is not about mind hacking or brainwashing; it's about the offer, giving value in exchange for your audiences' money, subscription, or trust. Having a better understanding of this will help expand your business and help you explore the realm of marketing that has never been touched.

The Persuasive Marketer is your best bet.

INTRODUCTION

Why is it that only a small fraction of businesses stay profitable and can withstand the storm that every other business face? The difference is the business owner's dedication and drive to build, sharpen, and apply the skills that matter as well as the ability to generate sales, which is the number one skill. Repeat customers and successful transactions are the lifeblood of your business -- the oxygen in which your business would die without their support. There is almost no business problem you cannot solve if you can grow your sales and generate more income.

As the owner, generating sales, therefore increasing your profit, is your number one goal. Making sales, on the side, is something you need to put more effort into and is not something that you can outsource or completely delegate. It is the most critical goal of any business. It does not matter if you have offered a fantastic product or service. The whole of your existence as an entrepreneur lives and dies by the effectiveness of your selling and marketing ability to produce new sales. The success of your business is not dependent on your inspiration, your staff, your passion, or your ability to support people. If you have a marketing and sales machine that predictably brings in tons of new customers every day, it can be so sweet to own a business.

Owning a business can be volatile, inefficient, and extremely stressful; that is because of your business' future profits, sustaining your family, your workers, and their families rest in whatever 'fate' drops down in your hands. You may choose to disregard this reality, turn a blind eye, and say to yourself that all is going to go well, or you can read this book from cover to cover and make sure your business isn't turning into a boring investment.

Either way, you have to realize that all the new shiny marketing strategies, hacks, and resources currently peddled won't solve your business' number one problem, which is, "How can I get more customers – and therefore more sales?"

I will tell you in this book things you will not learn anywhere else. The methods I reveal within are highly controversial, not that they are untrue. It is because they are more accurate than anything else you've ever learned about marketing and sales. Everything you will find in this book will change everything about you, and in particular, how you think about business, your audience, and your profits.

The truth is, much of the time a business owner spends on their business is always to grow it. However, selling should be your number one priority as a business owner, so you have to behave accordingly. It means focusing the majority of your time on marketing and sales activities. That does not mean you have to be the one on the line to make the sale yourself, nor does it mean that you have to submit every copy of your sales to your website. You have to be incredibly involved in every step of the sales and marketing process, so you can fully grasp the challenges and find the opportunities. It does not matter what skills you bring to your business, whether it is a problem solver, a fantastic planner, or a person with numbers or a person with systems and processing ideas to be a successful entrepreneur. You need to become the number one expert in selling for your business. There is only one way to do it, and that is to spend your time, attention, and energy in activity producing money -- or selling product.

CONCEPT OF MARKETING

If you're still trying to sell to people using old, worn out, hard closing strategies that worked decades ago, you're going to become extinct soon. You cannot trick a customer into selling something to them. No matter what you have learned from some online marketers and sales trainers, the mind control strategies are not required. Good commercialization is not coercion. By helping your clients and buyers, you will sell more and make more profits by not taking advantage of them.

You entered your business to serve others and make money, and that is why you'll love the strategies I'll share. These methods allow you to direct, promote, and provide value for your customers before they spend a single penny. Many times, my students send me messages, feeling so pleased that they appreciate the value I've shared with them, even though they haven't purchased any of my products or been part of my premium class. You do not have to wait before someone turns into a customer before bringing value into their lives.

Today's consumers are happier and more educated than ever, taking their time to study products, and contrasting yours with other rivals. They are also looking into the latest breakthroughs that occur in your area. A highly educated consumer will be a detrimental strike to you if you pursue old sales tactics focused on tricking people into buying your products or services. However, if you are focused on helping your customers, that's going to be a game-changer for you.

You may have heard the word 'content marketing' before, and you will see some relation along the line with the strategy discussed here. You can share content with your audience through emails, blogs, podcasts, videos, webinars, social media groups, and maybe even live presentations. You may have also attempted some of those methods, but the results you hoped for were still not achieved. Most content marketing is ineffective as it shares the wrong kind of content and has no systematic strategy behind it.

You must first define the type of audience you want to target before you begin publishing. Study the population of your audience -- where they live, in which industry they operate, where they get their knowledge, and most of all, what problems they currently face. When you analyze these things. In this way, the content you need to produce is decided to draw customers to your product. If you do not know, your readers can't click on your content.

Your audience has a problem they want to solve. People are genetically conditioned to make the least effort and profit in solving a problem. It is your role as a marketing professional to show them the best way to solve their problem economically. If you do, your website and your social media platforms will be on the road to increased organic traffic.

Whether it is on social media, on sites, or both, we who work online must find creative ways to market ourselves, our companies, and our products. We need a marketing definition, even though the word per se is not recognised or used. We all specialise in marketing and strive to do our best.

At the right time, we need to give the right message to the right audience, and this is not an easy task because no two people think and feel identical. Indeed, there are no two people in the world who are the same, so we have to work with general ideas for the public consumer.

Marketing transforms the investment relatively fast and returns it correctly when completed. You should consider designing your marketing concept to get there sooner rather than later and do the best of it.

Marketing is the processing of your products and services to exciting prospects and customers. The main word for this concept is "marketing," which includes analysis, promotion, sales, and distribution.

This is a significant problem because you can obtain a four-year marketing degree and write volumes on marketing and still get it all wrong. Essentially, marketing is all you do to pull together your goods and services.

Marketing is one of the company's most critical components. In addition to increasing brand recognition, marketing can also improve revenue, grow business, and attract customers.

The word "marketing" involves several activities related to the selling of the goods and services of your company. Advertising and consumer research, which better suits your product to the needs and wishes of the consumer, are the most evident marketing activity. Brand design is also a form of marketing as it helps to customize the goods and services of your business to suit established consumer needs. It is not merely an essential part of the performance of the business, and it is the business on its own. Everything else depends on marketing in the company.

Promoting is extremely helpful for the exchange, trade, and to traffic products. Merchandise and enterprises are made accessible to clients through different mediators, in particular wholesalers and retailers, and so forth. Showcasing is helpful for producers and customers.

The previous discussions about the particular needs and inclinations of shoppers and the last about the items that manufacturers and creators of products can offer include structuring items that are satisfactory to purchasers and completing exercises that encourage the exchange of possession between the merchant and the purchaser.

The exhibition of the advertising capacity is essential since it is the primary way that the organisation can create pay or salary and produce benefits. Any movement identified with pay age is a promoting measure. It is unreasonably simple for the bookkeeper, engineer, and so forth, working under the general suspicion that the organisation will have a complete deal volume of numerous dollars.

In any case, somebody must go to the market and get dollars from society to keep the business running, because, without these assets, the association will die. Promoting offers is one approach to make a benefit with purchasing and selling property by making proprietorship time, area, and utilities. These benefits and gains are reinvested in the gathering, which implies that more benefits will be made later on. Promoting must be critical since the endurance of the organisation relies upon the viability of the advertising capacity.

The Advertising method is a complex term; it has evolved in general. These shifts have far-reaching implications on both growth and sales. The marketing has to do the same, given the rapidly changing tastes and preferences of people.

Marketing as a measurement device provides room for recognising this new market trend, thus, creating and rendering available goods accordingly.

IMPORTANCE OF MARKETING

IT INFORMS

Marketing at a specific level is useful for teaching consumers. Yeah, you know the product's advantages and drawbacks, but do the consumers? To buy into a company, the customer wants a fundamental understanding of what a company does, what it offers, and how it works. Marketing is the most successful means of conveying your value proposition in a friendly and informative manner to your clients. If customer awareness is on your priority list, marketing will be on it as well.

IT EQUALISES

Digital marketing is cheaper than any other product. Social networking channels and e-mail promotions have made connecting to customers a lot more financially efficient.

Strategic marketing can also boost business opportunities for small and medium-sized companies by engaging with established rivals. In reality, marketing will offer even small and medium-sized businesses a push forward. SME executives also have even more time to pay personalised attention to each customer across various marketing channels, due to the smaller scale of their company. Modern shoppers appreciate the overpricing of the product over most prominent brands because this form of one-on-one engagement direct buyer towards you.

IT SUSTAINS

Marketing is primarily designed to sustain a company's visibility, not to address the lack of interaction. Marketing in this way is something that corporations seek to build and handle every day to ensure positive interactions with their customers. Marketing is critical because it helps businesses to establish long-term, pervasive relationships with their customers. It is not a one-stop approach but a continuing project that allows companies to succeed.

IT ENGAGES

Customer loyalty is the cornerstone of a profitable enterprise, which applies mainly to SMEs. When the customer exits the house, marketing answers the problem of how to carry on a conversation. External encounters in the past accounted for a significant part of B2C involvement. They go to the pizzeria, converse with the host, joke with the waitress, meet the owner, etc.

This is no longer enough as long as this emotional engagement continues. Consumers take themselves out of business. That is where messaging comes in so you will give material to your clients, regardless of the channel, to keep them occupied after business hours. Your customer needs to communicate with your brand, and this is why you can use ads.

IT SELLS

It's essential to market because it lets you promote your product or service. The bottom line in every company is money-making, and marketing is a crucial tool to achieve the ultimate objective. Most companies would not survive without marketing, as marketing eventually determines revenue. Sure, you must have a decent product, but if customers do not know your deals, how do you launch sales first? You cannot say it that way. SMEs need to develop enticing new products to lure and motivate consumers to shop. Marketing aids the company in boosting profits and revenues. What else can you wish for your business?

IT GROWS

Marketing is a vital tactic to ensure that your business is rising. While your new clients are always your highest priority, marketing strategies will help you grow that base. Small initiatives such as social media updates and e-mail promotions will benefit all current users and alert future new buyers as well. Marketing ultimately secures the company's prosperity with fresh and old customer satisfaction.

MISTAKES MADE BY MARKETERS

You will bind your business to the right clients through a successful marketing campaign, get people to talk about your business, show your product or service to the media and get your company in line with financial success. Reflective marketing may also do the opposite.

Marketing errors will result in a significant loss of income and other expenses for your business. Marketing errors can sometimes even lead to a problem with public relations.

Did you know it does not have to be complicated or expensive to market your business? You can generate significant interest in your business with a little imagination that can create more traffic, more customers, and more revenue.

Although many entrepreneurs think these results are brilliant, particularly to a beer budget, they also make foolish marketing mistakes that can be easily avoided.

LACK OF RESEARCH AND TESTING

Testing and lack of research about the product and marketing trends are some of the most common marketing mistakes made by businesses.

Market analysis and testing save time and money by assessing how the goods and promotions perform before any campaign launch. They have an overview of how the public views marketing strategies. This helps you recognise weak or controversial ideas before you take responsibility for their implementation.

Make sure you understand how customers react to your marketing efforts. Develop several bids, rates, packages, and deals, and then see how potential clients respond to each bid.

IMPROPER FOCUS AND POSITIONING

Brand placement is an essential factor in developing and separating the company from the competition. Strategic market positioning provides traction, which means that it builds on the old product any time you launch a new product or service.

Most firms, however, market single goods without caring about the general image of their brand. So any marketing campaign that requires time, money, and energy will begin again.

Avoid these marketing mistakes by using positioning tactics to affect your way of contrasting consumers with your competitors. Are you planning on luxury items? Are the goods a condition for you? Are you known for high quality or a customer type?

The entire approach and positioning of every product or service you market will rely on these answers, which creates a particular niche where you can develop a loyal consumer base for your industry.

MARKETING WITHOUT A UNIQUE SELLING POINT

The only argument that separates you from the competition is your exclusive selling bid -- your selling proposal will demonstrate, like no other company does, how the benefits of your company meet customer needs directly.

Doesn't someone else solve a problem? Build a low-priced luxury quality? Do you have any lifestyle to sell? Are you using new and appropriate products or resources?
Customers need exposure to various marketing messages. It is likely your business will be lost in the noise if you don't give them a USP.

Stop this marketing error by making all marketing decisions based on your USP. It helps clients understand why and what separates them from their rivals.

FAILING TO CAPTURE REPEAT CUSTOMERS

The reliance on new clients and the lack of recurring business income is a growing marketing mistake.

It is necessary to acquire new customers but not as lucrative for customers who are returning. Sales to a new customer on average are five times costlier than sales to a current customer.

Before purchasing, a frequent customer has to conquer fewer hurdles because he already had faith in their business. Moreover, the higher the probability of a consumer buying from you again.

You are losing a significant part of the market when the marketing campaigns only reach new customers. Avoid this marketing mistake by using several tools to track repeat purchasers to attract new purchasers.

LACK OF FOCUS ON POTENTIAL CUSTOMERS' NEEDS

How well are you familiar with your customers and their problems? Surprisingly, few businesses take the time to figure out what their consumers want and need.

It's a simple but not an easy secret to avoid this common mistaken. Find a need which you can meet and then fulfil it better than your competitors.

You must perform work and testing to understand these criteria. Once you know what consumers want, a competitive USP can be produced that places the brand on the market in general. So, you can win back customers quickly if you know just what your customers need and want.

Even with the best planning, marketing mistakes will occur. If you have no marketing strategy to address, take the time to think about what has gone wrong and how to position yourself more effectively in the future. It is time to focus once more on recognising and reacting to customers ' needs if your company struggles with marketing.

PERSUASIVE MARKETING

Te effect of the human mind and behavioral characteristics have strong pivotal roles on the way they respond to propositions from others without being disadvantaged in any way; various in-built mindsets acquired over time based on cultural, psychological, emotional and ethnic persuasions have an impact on the response of people to information from other people which subject them to complexities that is difficult to predict. However, solutions are not far-fetched as quite some copious numbers of studies have inputted in understanding human psychology, which could be applied to enhance marketing in all of its forms.

Unpredictable communication and decision-making occur at the subconscious level, requiring marketers to consider the psychological underpinnings of attractive and purchasing behaviour, which is facilitated by understanding the factors that apply at this level. They can be far more effective at persuading people to choose what they want them to choose and purchase.

Persuasion marketing is a strong and indispensable tool for massive sales in marketing. What then is persuasion marketing? Persuasion marketing applies what we know about human psychology to develop techniques to market products or services. In this case, it intricately applies to the promotion aspect of the marketing mix and builds on a customer's cognitive, behavioral, emotional, mental characteristics to lead them to purchase. It applies to what is known about human psychology to develop attractive strategies to market products or services. In this case, it specifically refers to the promotion aspect of the marketing mix and builds on a customer's impulsive behavior to lead them to purchase.

More so, it is defined as the study and practice of marketing with the view that as humans, we think we're rational. However, that's all an illusion because observation and research show our decisions are influenced entirely by irrational ways that go unnoticed. The use of persuasive marketing has been engaged in different electoral processes to predict the outcome of the election based on the psychological and impulsive mechanisms of candidates during campaigns. Persuasion marketing uses the concept that people can make rational purchase decisions some of the time, but much of the time, they don't. Instead, people make decisions based on emotion and factors that are not logical reasons, like the fact that other people have brought the product. Furthermore, the most interesting anecdote about persuasion marketing is that it works even if you are aware of how it works.

It is unarguable in marketing that the effect of communication cannot be overemphasised as it is the heart of persuasive marketing. By mirroring a target's gestures and physical postures while engaging casual conversation, you can develop an unuttered bond with that target, making them feel that you two are "in sync." After that, introduce your gesture. If the target copies your gesture, you know you've gone from following to leading. Only now can you insert your ideas in conversation, hopefully extracting the beautiful response of, "That's just what I was thinking."

The Internet is a significant component of digital commerce; persuasion marketing includes how a web page is strategically structured. That is, applying human psychology to web design by focusing on the part of the decision-making process that's not consciously controlled, elements such as layout, copy, and typography, combined with the right promotional messages, encourage website visitors to follow pre-planned pathways on the website, and take specific actions, instead of giving them a free course of choice in how they interact with the website.

According to research, questions have been asked as to who uses persuasive marketing most with statistically influenced results stating that "salespeople have been using persuasive techniques for as long as they have been exposed, and now work to translate these techniques on the web. Persuasion marketing was a top subject discussed by keynote speaker Susan Bratton at the 2011 SES (Search

Engine Strategies) San Francisco convention, attended by more than 1,000 marketing and advertising professionals. It's a topic and a strategic approach that appeals to marketers in a variety of industries, especially in e-commerce."

Due to advancement in technology, globalisation, and electronic communication have further eroded the traditional system as ideas and people flow more freely than ever around organisations and as decisions get made closer to the markets. These fundamental realities change more than a decade in the making but now are firmly part of the economic terrain, which essentially comes down to this -- work today gets done in an environment where people don't just ask, "What should I do? But also, why should I do it?"

To answer this why question effectively, is to persuade. Yet many businesspeople misunderstand persuasion and more still underutilise it. The reason for this is that persuasion is widely perceived as a skill reserved for selling products and closing deals. It is also commonly seen as another form of manipulation-devious and to be avoided. Persuasion can be used in selling and deal-clinching situations, and it can be misused to manipulate people. However, exercised constructively and to its full potential, persuasion supersedes sales and is quite the opposite of deception.

The ideology of persuasion, like that of power, often confuses and even mystifies businesspeople due to its complex nature-and so dangerous when mishandled-that many would rather just avoid it altogether. However, like power, persuasion can be a force for enormous good in marketing. It can pull people together, craft remedies, move ideas forward, galvanise change, and forge constructive solutions. To do all that, people must understand persuasion for what it is not convincing and selling but learning and negotiating. In furtherance, it must be seen as an art form that requires commitment and constant practice, especially as today's business contingencies make persuasion more necessary than ever.

PERSUASION IS A LEARNING PROCESS

Frankly speaking, persuasion involves moving people to a position they don't currently hold; and not by cajoling or deceiving. Instead, it requires careful preparation, the proper framing of arguments, the presentation of vivid supporting evidence, and the effort to find the correct emotional match with your audience. Effective persuasion is a time-consuming and challenging proposition. Still, it may also be more potent than the command-and-control managerial model it succeeds, which does not support frictionless relationships in business parlance.

According to Lawrence Bossidy, "The day when you could shout and scream and beat people into good performance is over. Today you have to appeal to them by helping them see how they can get from here to there, by establishing some credibility, and by giving them some reason and help to get there. Do all those things, and they'll knock down doors."

In essence, he described persuasion now more than ever, as the language of business leadership. Effective persuasion becomes a negotiating and learning process through which a persuader leads people to a problem's shared solution.

How then is persuasion a learning process? Persuasion is a learning and negotiating process in the most general terms. It involves phases of discovery, preparation, and negotiation. Getting ready to persuade clients can take weeks or months of planning as you learn about your audience and the position you intend to argue. Before they even start to talk, effective persuaders have considered their positions from every possible angle. What investments in time and money will my position require from others? Is my supporting evidence weak in any way? Are there alternative positions I need to examine?

Dialogue happens before and during the persuasion process before it begins to get you results.

Effective persuaders use dialogue to learn more about their audience's opinions, concerns, and perspectives of thoughts. During the process, dialogue continues to be a form of learning, but it is also the beginning of the negotiation stage. You invite people to discuss, even debate, the merits of your products or services, and then to offer honest feedback and suggest alternative solutions.

That may sound like a slow way to achieve your goal, but effective persuasion is about testing and revising ideas in concert with your clients' concerns and needs. The best persuaders not only listen to others but also incorporate their perspectives into a shared solution. Persuasion, in other words, often involves indeed and demands compromise. Perhaps that is why the most effective persuaders seem to share a common trait -- they are open-minded, never dogmatic. They enter the persuasion process prepared to adjust their viewpoints and incorporate others' ideas, especially yours.

This persuasion approach interestingly is highly persuasive in itself. When clients see that a persuader is eager to hear their views and willing to make changes in response to their needs and concerns, they respond very positively. They trust the persuader more and listen more attentively. They don't fear being bowled over or manipulated. They see the persuader as flexible and are thus more willing to make sacrifices themselves. That is such a powerful dynamic, that good persuaders often enter the persuasion process with judicious compromises already prepared.

UNDERSTANDING MENTAL DIFFERENCES IN PEOPLE

DEALING WITH SCEPTICS

No matter how hard you try to convince people to believe in what you are bringing to them, it is not uncommon to find a few people who will not just comply with believing in your product marketing. These are called "Sceptics." The most defining trait of sceptics is that they tend to have very strong personalities. They can be rebellious, demanding, disruptive, disagreeable, and even antisocial. They may have a combative style and are usually described as take-charge people. They tend to be self-absorbed and act primarily on their feelings.

The amazing thing about them is that you will know almost immediately where you converse with sceptics. You can almost always depend on them to tell you what they are thinking because of their strong personalities. To persuade a sceptic, you need as much credibility as you can garner. Sceptics tend to trust people who are similar to them-for instance, people who went to the same college, engage in the same activities and hobbies, or worked for the same companies.

To win the heart of a sceptic, you would need to find him lay credence to your personality, products, and services. Credibility can be transferred (from a colleague, for instance), but ultimately it must be earned, and you may have to go through some very aggressive questioning to establish it. If you haven't established needed credibility with a sceptic, you need to find a way to have it transferred to you before or during the meeting for example, by gaining an endorsement from someone the sceptic trusts. This is a chain method of reaching out to the soul of the sceptic; implementing this will let the sceptic maintain their superior position while allowing you to discuss issues on their level openly.

DEALING WITH A SCEPTIC

The first rule is never to challenge a sceptic, it is risky and must be handled delicately. Sometimes, to make your case, you will need to correct bad information that the sceptic is relying on, but this also must be done wisely without killing their ego. In other words, when you need to correct a sceptic, give them room to save face; never burst their bubbles! For them to trust you, they need to maintain their reputation, and ego - this is their problem from the onset.

More so, do not forget that sceptics do not like being helped; they prefer having people think they know something already-their ignorant side must not be punctured. Although persuading a sceptic might sound daunting, the process is very straightforward. Sceptics want to move forward with groundbreaking ideas, but they first need to make sure that those ideas are from people they fully trust. Sceptics usually make decisions quickly within days, if not right on the spot. Magic words to use with a sceptic include feel, grasp, power, action, suspicion, trust, agreeable, demand, and disrupt.

DEALING WITH FOLLOWERS

These sets of people are simple-hearted; they find it very easy to see from other perspectives and tend to quickly believe one's persuasive techniques without much effort. Because they are afraid of making the wrong choice, followers will seldom be early adopters. They trust in known brands and in bargains, both of which represent less risk.

They are also very good at seeing the world through other people's eyes, even though they are cautious, yet they are seldom spontaneous in taking decisions. Above all, though, they are responsible for decision-makers, which is why they are most often found in large corporations. Followers account for more than a third of all the people interested in a package, goods or services.

The characteristics given to followers does not necessarily mean they are dull-hearted. Followers may engage you in long lists of issues and repeatedly challenge your position on the validity of a product (similar to what a sceptic does), but don't be deceived. In the end, they will agree to something only if they've seen it done elsewhere. However, followers won't admit this. They will seldom concede that they are followers; they would much rather have you believe that they are innovative and forward-thinking. Frequently, followers are mistaken for sceptics. However, followers are not intrinsically suspicious; they prefer that you help them gain a better comprehension of what they don't understand. Although followers may exhibit a take-charge approach, they will yield when challenged. That's the extent of their simplicity. As a general rule, people who are difficult to classify into a decision-making style are usually followers.

HOW TO DEAL WITH FOLLOWERS

Although followers are often the most difficult to identify, they can be the easiest to persuade if you know which buttons to push in relating to them. To obtain buy-in from a follower, you need to make him feel confident about deciding to move in a particular direction by proving that others have succeeded on that path. Not surprisingly, followers tend to focus on proven methods, and references and testimonials are big persuading factors. With a follower, don't try to sell yourself unless you have a strong track record of success, they don't in a gullible manner accept your person but the integrity of your products.

Instead, look for past decisions by the follower that support your views or find similar decisions by other executives the follower trusts. Ideally, followers want solutions that are innovative yet proven, new but trusted, leading-edge yet somewhat safe. This is why they rarely make out-of-the-box decisions because they are logical thinkers with a holistic view. In fact, for some followers, the only way to persuade them to adopt a bold strategy is to get someone else to do it successfully first. Buzzwords and phrases to use with a follower include innovate, expedite, swift, bright, just like before, expertise, similar to, previous, what works, and old way.

DEALING WITH CHARISMATICS

Charismatics are hyperactive but don't take action easily. They want to move quickly from the big idea to the specifics-especially those details regarding implementation. Charismatics are often described as enthusiastic, captivating, talkative, dominant, and persistent. They are risk-seeking yet responsible individuals. They are impressed with intelligence and facts and not usually given to self-absorption and compulsiveness. Although charismatics may show great abundance for a new idea, getting a final commitment from them can be difficult.

They've learned from experience, particularly from the bad decisions they've made, to temper their initial enthusiasm with a good dose of reality. They seek out facts and figures to support their emotions, and if such data can't be proven or found, they will quickly lose their enthusiasm for that idea.

They are hardly convinced by one-sided arguments that lack a strong orientation toward results. Eventually, charismatics make their final decisions very methodically, and the choices are based on balanced information.

HOW TO HANDLE CHARISMATICS

In your bid to persuade a charismatic, you need to fight the urge to join in their excitement, which might deceitfully fool you to let off your perseverance and guard. One approach is to slightly undersell the parts of your proposal that pique their interest. In other words, you should be prepared to merely acknowledge the items that he greets with enthusiasm and discuss the risks of each of those things. When you do, this will ground your proposal in reality and strengthen their confidence and trust in you as well as increase their curiosity. You also need to keep the discussion focused on results and never waver into unnecessary arguments. Your arguments must be simple and straightforward, and you should use visual aids to stress the features and benefits of your proposal. If you don't provide this results-oriented information, even when it's not asked for), you risk that the charismatic will not have it later when he needs it.

Furthermore, you should be very honest and up-front about the risks involved with accepting your proposal, while also delineating the measures that can help minimise those risks. If you try to conceal any potential downsides, you can be sure that the charismatic will discover them later when you're not available to address any concerns he may have.

All executives are busy people, but the attention span of a charismatic can be particularly short. In a meeting, you need to start with the most critical information. Otherwise, you risk losing their attention if you take your time leading up to a crucial point. Charismatics expect you to patiently wait for them to make a decision, which could take some time, even though their initial enthusiasm may have led you to believe otherwise. Magic words that can help hold a charismatic's interest include results, proven actions, show, watch, look, bright, easy, clear, and focus.

ELEMENTS OF PERSUASIVE MARKETING

There are four major elements applied in achieving persuasive marketing, which would be potent enough to break down any ethnic, cultural, emotional, or behavioural structures built as defence mechanisms against the allowance of others' opinions, suggestions, or information. By building these persuasion marketing skills, it would be easy to achieve your aim in massive sales. These are:

Structured communication: This is also known as "planned conversation" of interpersonal sales to strategically lure human psychology into believing and opening their heart to receive the marketing. It is about controlling the order of the dialogue, or how information is presented to the consumer. The strategy is to move a customer along his or her "impulse curve," which invariably means the use of customer's strength to have access into their approval by initially encouraging a customer's impulse, and making a call to action after that impulse level has been raised to its highest point. In website design, it means that the first page the customer sees does not immediately seek a sale, but instead presents the initial information and encourages further exploration of the website.

What kinds of customers are they where structured communication is effective?

One of the insights of persuasion marketing is that customers' sensitivity to persuasive arguments varies according to several factors, including their immediate emotional state. Therefore, to wisely increase the chances of converting a customer, a salesperson or marketer needs to look for a "persuasion window," open one if they can, and make the deal before it closes again.

 For instance, consider a visitor who has just registered for a newsletter on an e-Commerce website and lands on a "Thank You" page. Since that visitor has already engaged with the website and is in an "interactive state," additional offers on "Thank You" pages typically earn a 39 percent conversion rate, ensuring that the client is kept in conversion triggering the retentive memory of the customer as regards the products or services.

In another case, to generate persuasive windows is to "alarm clock" a website. Many marketers design pages in a way that people have reasons to regularly check it to avoid "missing out" on opportunities or offers. When people visit a website on their own time, they come back already open to persuasion.

Neuro-marketing: Neuro-marketing is perhaps, according to many as the most important component of persuasion marketing, applying psychology to the marketing message, which is based on the fact that major logical reasoning takes place here. Psychological research reveals information about the diverse factors that contribute to a decision and as much as 90 percent of that all takes place beyond our conscious reasoning.

For example, research demonstrates that visual and olfactory cues are important for "priming" a particular mood; therefore, grocery stores display flowers in the front to "prime" customers with the image of freshness. In terms of website design, it means using a colour scheme and particular visual imagery to improve visitors' responses to the website.

The power of testimony from other people can within the twinkle of an eye massively direct people and sales to your products. Some marketing managers are professional in typically displaying customer testimony on their websites, developing a "wall of social proof" approach. Businesses post photos of happy, satisfied, and attract customers, so new customers are comfortable being associated with them.

Storytelling: Due to the innate desire of people to hear something new and the relaxing aura it releases on human consciousness; it, therefore, confers an attracting bait on people to use a narrative framework to invoke a customer's emotional and subconscious responses, so that they join or dominate their more analytical responses. When in a good mood, the world doesn't make sense when indebted to favour can (or must) take immediate action right after a mistake, right after being denied a request. Use of particular words and images evoke habitual emotional responses, such as affection, empathy, familiarity, and desire for triumph/resolution. After that, reciprocation obligates people emotionally by giving them a sense of commitment, which could then be built upon; people don't want to back out on the initial commitment, so they are more likely to comply with new proofs.

Therefore, it is important to be friendly and physically attractive. Never show ugly people in your pictures in your digital narrative mechanisms.

Stories that intimately relate to your audience to strengthen your brand position is always necessary. If your story doesn't have this, your copy will come off cheesy. The story works because it is relevant to an ideal buyer and product as concise and straightforward imagery is concrete and vivid. Your job is to tell an unexpected story that will entertain your ideal customer. Something they won't read on an Amazon product description.

Copywriting: Copywriting is the mechanism of using the right words and phrases for headings, captions, product descriptions, and other texts to compel people to engage in sales. For instance, when people scan material, and most Internet pages are scanned before being read, questions stand out more than statements. So, phrases like, "What is the best method to capture attention?" catches more attention than "How to capture attention."

The use of the power words "best method" captures the attention even in an unconscious manner. The persuasion marketer field-tests different kinds of copy, to determine which is most likely to produce the emotion or answer he or she's looking for. Different words describing the same thing can have a very different connotation. "Choices," for example, produces a positive emotional response, but "trade-offs" produces a negative one. Additionally, the copywriter and marketer must remember that the fear of loss is more motivating for most people than the promise of gain. Thus "don't miss out" has more impact than "this can be yours."

THE TECHNIQUES OF PERSUASIVE MARKETING

Having established the basic elements of persuasive marketing, the powerful combination of the elements, as mentioned earlier with techniques, would bring about an irresistible potency to capture a copious number of sales.

Persuasive marketing techniques that you can implement to boost your promotional efforts, depending on your industry, business, product, service, or other goals, apply to any kind of global marketing by studying the peculiarity of your products, services to the marketing system involved.

HAVE GOOD RELATIONSHIP WITH PEOPLE

A relationship or a prior relationship with someone could have a substantial effect on their approval or disapproval of your products and services. The relationship matters a lot in breaking through in the sphere of e-commerce or any kind of business marketing as people tend to do business with someone they trust rather than someone they do not. Ninety percent of people give their commitment to others or firms they have tested, trusted, and built a cordial relationship with over time. For instance, think of the last time you were asked to do something for someone. Did the fact that you did or didn't like them play into your decision making about them and propositions? If so, then use that as a lesson in why you need to be likeable.

This is another aspect of stringed relationships in commitment to information in that persuasion can be extremely effective when it comes from peers. Science supports what most sales professionals already know -- testimonials from satisfied customers work best when the satisfied customer and the prospective customer share similar circumstances. That lesson can help a manager faced with the task of selling a new corporate initiative. Imagine that you're trying to streamline your department's work processes. A group of veteran employees is resisting. Rather than try to convince the employees of the move's merits yourself, ask an old-timer who supports the initiative to speak up for it at a team meeting. The compatriot's testimony stands a much better chance of convincing the group than yet another speech from the boss. Simply stated, influence is often best exerted horizontally rather than vertically.

It's a lot easier for someone to say yes to someone likeable than to someone who is not. A few ideas for being likeable when trying to increase sign-ups and to increase sales during a webinar include, but aren't limited to:

1. Focus on them, not you. – If you focus too much on yourself, you instantly or eventually come off as a person who cares more about yourself than your potential customers.

2. Give the information before ever mentioning a sales pitch. – Make yourself vulnerable to serving the people around you as much as you can, since webinar hosts who open with a sales pitch or even talk about the products and services they will be selling at the end are far less likeable than those that first focus on serving their audience.

3. Simplify things, but don' talk down to your audience. – People tend to like simplicity than complexity since they, themselves, are complex in their nature and thinking. While you may understand all your industry jargon, your audience might not. Therefore, you should explain things in a way they will comprehend the concepts you are teaching. At the same time, do your best not to talk down to them because that will turn them off from you in a flash.

4. Do well to answer questions and take the time to acknowledge your audience. – People in their naturalness want to feel seen and heard. If you're live, start by asking people to chime in with where

they're tuning in from, and what they hope to get out of watching.

ENGAGE EMOTIONAL INTELLIGENCE

Emotion is a sense of feeling as people are moved by what and how they think of that first appealing to reason, especially for those who are not careful and disciplined about their sense of affection and pleasure. For example, have you noticed that a lot of commercials, sales pages, and ads tell a nice story? The story of someone, just like you who has a problem similar to the one that you have, a problem that caused them to suffer. Then they found the solution to that problem, and it changed their lives. Even though the problem is not where they are going, but a means to show they understand how you feel about the problem sympathetically. They trigger your sense of having ease, comfort, and pleasure, which is almost impossible to deny.

Therefore, to drive charitable donations and voluminous sales, this is one of those persuasive marketing techniques that aligns the heartstrings with the purse strings. The feeling that their life can be changed too; the feeling that their problem can be solved also, compels them to buy. It's why it's so important to get your audience emotionally involved with your content, your products, or your services. If you can make people feel like your solution is the one that will not only help but also change their situation, then yours is the one they are going to buy into.

Great persuaders are aware of the primacy of emotions and are responsive to them in two important ways:

1) They show their emotional commitment to the position they are advocating. Such expression is an essential matter in persuasive marketing. Despite that, you must not act too emotional; people may doubt your genuineness. However, you must also show that your commitment to a goal is not just in your mind but in your heart and gut as well; you must carry it all over your system to show your heart is dedicated to the course. Without this demonstration of feeling and passion, people may wonder if you believe in the position you're championing.

Sometimes that would mean coming on strong, with forceful points able to convince your clients. Other times, a whisper may be all that is required. The idea is that whatever your position, you match your emotional enthusiasm to your audience's ability to receive the message. More importantly, however, is that effective persuaders have a strong and accurate understanding of their audience's emotional state, and they adjust the tone of their arguments accordingly.

2) Effective persuaders seem to have a second sense about how their colleagues have related past events in the organisation and how they will probably interpret a proposal. The best persuaders in our study would usually canvass key individuals who had a good pulse on the mood and emotional expectations of those about to be persuaded. They would ask those individuals how diverse proposals might affect colleagues on an emotional level-in essence, testing possible reactions. They were also quite effective at gathering information through informal conversations in the hallways or at lunch. In the end, they aim to ensure that the emotional appeal behind their

persuasion matches what their audience is already feeling or expecting. This understanding aids you in moving away from emotional manipulation that could hinder your colleagues from trusting you in subsequent times.

BUILD TRUST

It is almost impossible for an effective persuader to advocate a new or contrarian position without having people wonder, "Can we trust this individual's perspectives and opinions?" Such a reaction is understandable. After all, allowing oneself to be persuaded is risky because any new initiative demands a commitment of time, energy, and resources. Regardless, even though persuaders must have high credibility, our research strongly suggests that most managers overestimate their credibility-considerably. In the workplace, credibility grows out of two sources -- expertise and relationships. People are considered having high levels of expertise if they have a history of sound judgment or have proven themselves knowledgeable and well informed about their proposals. For example, in proposing a new product idea, an effective persuader would need to be perceived as possessing a thorough understanding of the product-its specifications, target markets, customers, and competing products. A history of prior successes would further strengthen the persuader's perceived expertise. A work well done before and good reputation of a persuader would confer trust for subsequent times, which means people with high credibility have demonstrated-again, usually over time that they can be trusted to listen and to work in the best interests of others. They have also consistently shown strong emotional character, accountability, reliability, and integrity; that is, they are not known for mood extremes or inconsistent performance. Indeed, people who are known to be honest, steady, and reliable have an edge when going into any persuasion situation. Because their relationships are robust, they are more apt to be given the benefit of the doubt.

You must note that expertise and relationships determine credibility; you must undertake a sincere assessment of where you stand on both criteria before beginning the persuasive journey. To do so, first, step back and ask yourself the following questions related to expertise.

- How will others perceive my knowledge about the product, or what change would the product have?
- Do I have a track record in this area that others know about and respect?
- Then, to assess the strength of your relationship's credibility, ask yourself, do those I am hoping to persuade see me as helpful, trustworthy, and supportive?
- Will they see me as someone in sync with them- emotionally, intellectually, and politically on issues like this one?
- Finally, it is important to note that it is not enough to get your read on these matters. You must also test your answers with colleagues you trust to give you a reality check. Only then will you have a complete picture of your credibility.

In most cases, that exercise helps people discover that they have some measure of weakness, either on the expertise or on the relationship side of credibility.

BUILD ANTICIPATION

Curiosity is an element of making people hear you out and wait to hear you give a piece of information; even if the information is not the best of all, the heart position you have placed the person based on the fact that you have in a way excited and psyched them into believing an awesome package is coming erases the sense of reason. Therefore, start your marketing efforts by piquing their intent interest. Share some teasers before you make a big announcement. If you're not sure how to do it, take the lead from the movies and major brands. No one releases a movie or a new product without creating excitement around the film. They get people excited through short yet memorable messaging.

In a situation where you are about to launch a new blog post, lead magnet, e-Book, product, service, or webinar, the first persuasive technique you can use is to build anticipation. You don't want to spring something new on your audience and make them decide if it's something they want right at that moment.

Employ the same principle for your next launch. Get people excited about it so that by the time you launch, they are chomping at the bit to consume. For instance, "Next week in our masterclass, we're sharing effective five methods of rapid weight loss. Be sure to sign up for our webinar to get our supplement cheat sheet and workbook so you can follow along with us!"

The reason this is one of the best persuasive marketing techniques is that by whetting the appetite of your readers, not only will they be excited to sign up for the class, but they may also head to your website to see if they can glean any knowledge ahead of the event. It may be an excellent concept to add links for your top blog posts or even products and services to your registration page to get some website visits and purchases before your webinar occur.

TELL A NICE STORY

Storytelling has been touched on in the four major elements of persuasive marketing. Stories are one of the most powerful ways we communicate and pass information across. Human nature likes stories because they engage retrospective analysis of what could have happened in the past to draw a moral lesson. When we communicate through stories, we tap into a built-in power based on thousands of years of history. From time immemorial, humans have relied on the power of stories to both entertain and teach. When we employ stories, we are profiting from that history.

You can use stories for all different purposes, including to break through objections, teach, inspire, and so on. No efficient strategy is as easy to use or as powerful as the power of storytelling.

APPEAL TO LOGIC

Men love to reason things out critically. At times, based on the class of people you are dealing with, especially those with high intellectual quotient, it is better to focus less on emotions and more on logic in your business; use that as one of your persuasive marketing techniques. It's hard to argue with logic, and if your customers can't argue with your offer, they will find it hard to refuse. For example, everyone needs toothpaste. So how do you make sure your brand is the one that most people choose? Make sure yours is the one recommended by your country Dental Association.

Logically speaking, it is tough and impossible to argue with a recommendation by the organisation of dental health? Not selling toothpaste? Then find out who the authorities are in your industry and find a way to be certified by them. That will ensure that your business's solutions are the ones that are the logical choices in your industrial world.

PROOFS SPEAK LOUDER

In the sight of shreds of evidence of the efficiency of your product, it is easy to convince people unapologetically. You can't blame people for not taking advantage of something if there is nothing to back it up. This is why you need tangible proof(s) to share with your potential customers. This evidence could come in a statistical manner or testimonials from specific clients. Provide numerical data with examples, stories, metaphors, and analogies to make their positions come alive. That use of language paints a vivid word picture and, in doing so, lends a compelling and tangible quality to the persuader's point of view.

Ordinary verbal reports are too abstract to be completely meaningful or memorable. In essence, the numbers don't make an emotional impact. By contrast, stories and vivid language do, particularly when they present comparable situations to the one under discussion. A marketing manager trying to persuade senior executives to invest in a new product, for example, might cite examples of efficiency and fruitfulness of such products and services that paid off handsomely. Indeed, we found that people readily draw lessons from such cases. More importantly, the research shows that listeners absorb information in proportion to its vividness.

Few persuasive marketing techniques are as effective as real people using their real names and faces to sing the praises of whatever it is that you're selling. If you can't share testimonials, then share photos of before and after.

If people don't want to present themselves due to some cultural reasons or reasons known to them, you can start by being your customer. Use yourself as a case study. Alternatively, find some people you trust to try your product or service in exchange for them giving their review of it. Once you have the proof, persuading your audience to buy will be more straightforward.

COUNTERACT OBJECTIONS

To encourage someone to do something, you have to get past the roadblocks in their mind about it. Those objections might be myths, or they may be factual. They may feel like something is going to be too hard to implement when the reality is that it wouldn't be. They may feel like something is too expensive when the reality is that it will save them more in the long run by weighing the benefits against the cost.

Take, for instance, if you have been selling something for a while, you probably have received a lot of your customer's common objections through pre-sales messages, e-mails, and phone calls. Address those as a part of your marketing message. Persuade people by letting them know they can benefit from your products and services and spell out how.

For example, let's say you're delivering a webinar about using your social media angle to increase your customers' outreach online. If the concern is that it will be too difficult to use your software, you could walk them through how fast and easy it is to set up as part of your webinar, or you could offer a free tutorial and account set up with the purchase.

USING THE "FOMO" PRINCIPLE

There is a major principle of instilling the fear of losing by the disapproval of your package; this is known as FOMO (fear of missing out). It's popular because it's true; no one wants to miss out on anything. Phrases like "Only the first 25 people to buy will get this discount," "Limited supplies remaining," or "We're retiring this product at the end of this month," tell your audience there is a limit on how many units of your product are available.

Scarcity is one of the best persuasive marketing methods because it renders people agitated to immediately opt-in for the package in that if someone thinks it's their last chance to buy something, either for a long time or forever, they are going to take a little less time to weigh other options. In other words, they will have less time to think or talk themselves out, deciding to purchase as soon as possible.

In a nutshell, make something scarce. Whether it's the full product or service you're selling, or just a package, unit or bonus, make it something that only immediate action takers can get. The anxiety and curiosity your customers will have of not getting one of the last deals or specials can increase your sales massively.

CREATE A SENSE OF URGENCY

There are some persons who you might not be able to apprehend with the sense of scarcity due to their strong will to make a decision at their convenient time and more so if you're not a fan of scarcity, go with urgency persuasion instead. This allows you to keep selling your product or service indefinitely but makes the buyer feel they have to buy it sooner than later to enjoy the benefits the product or service will give them.

This simply connotes that if you have listed the main benefit of your product or service, remind people that the longer they wait to make a purchase, the longer it will be before they can feel the satisfaction of having that benefit, and the longer they wait; the more people will experience it before them.

In a simple example, imagine you're selling a meditation audio that will improve the quality of your customer's sleep. Your urgency copy could include phrases like "Don't go another night without restful sleep" or "Do you want to spend more sleepless nights tossing and turning?"

And maybe the product or service you're promoting in your webinar provides better health, life-changing experience, a richer wallet, or something similar. You can make that a part of your urgency messaging too. Tell your customers that they can't afford to wait any longer to purchase your product or service. After all, the longer they wait, the longer they will stay unhealthy or stay broke.

PRINCIPLE OF RECIPROCITY

There is a common saying that "Respect is reciprocal." This explains why people tend to do something for you when, in time past, you have also helped them. Do you know why so many people share such great information for free in blog posts, e-Books, lead magnets, and other forms of content? Because interchange is one of the strongest persuasive marketing techniques, when you do something nice for someone, they feel obligated to reciprocate. Praise is likely to have a warmth and softening effect on people because everyone is subject to the universal human tendency to treat people the way they treat them. If you have ever caught yourself smiling at a coworker just because he or she smiled first, you know how this principle works.

What this means in the business parlance is that the more discounts and free stuff you give to someone, your customers, the more indebted they feel towards you. So, when you pitch them your product or service, they will be more likely to buy it because they already feel like they owe you for the great free information you have given them so far. Help me, and I help you is what this process entails.

The more reason why creating highly informative webinars for your business is a winning marketing strategy. Throughout the webinar, you are giving value to your participants. At the end of the webinar, they should feel the need to reciprocate by purchasing, so they have paid for the value they have received along with the value they will later receive from their purchase.

INCITING CONTROVERSY TECHNIQUE

Nothing gets people's emotions on high like controversy. While it's a tough line to balance, if you can find the right way to get controversy into your marketing, you can compel an audience that is not only going to be pulled into your marketing but who is also going to talk about it wherever they go, thereby serving as a publicity mechanism of acceptance for your firm.

Controversy regarding your business competitors is something a lot of businesses like to take advantage of in the beginning. Local dentists let people know they didn't like to hunt when Walter Parson's received national outrage for his extracurricular activities. Hosting companies created "We Love Elephants" discounts and messaging to flow with the outrage Bob Parsons of *GoDaddy* received when he went elephant hunting. This is why it's a good idea always to follow and monitor the news about your competitors.

When one gets in trouble, no matter what the reason, you will likely find a bunch of new customers willing to come to you if you jump on the controversial bandwagon as your competitor's opposition.

PRINCIPLE OF COMMON GROUNDS AND ENEMY

It is very interesting if you and your potential customers or clients have a common enemy you could denounce before them so you could be more trusted to fight the same thing breeding a sense of mutual benefits. Have you ever noticed how easy it is to form a bond with someone through mutual dislike? That can be applied to your marketing.

When you are communicating with your audience, it's important to denounce the enemies you have in common. For example, if you're selling search engine optimisation (SEO) services, you can easily denounce the big-guy *Google* for their changes in rules that make it even harder for small businesses to get traffic from search engines without having to pay for advertising. The result is small business owners will agree with you that *Google* is making things difficult for them. They will feel like you do apprehend their heartfelt outcry, and they will trust you to help them fight the common enemy together through the use of your services. Instead of making them feel like you are their service provider, you will make them feel like you are their partner in crime.

This is in a way similar to the inciting controversy technique. However, you'll want to use caution with this one. Though you might be ready to pounce on the "enemy," your audience may see through that as an inauthentic ploy to get their money. It can certainly work, but you just have to tread this path of persuasive marketing carefully.

Even if your credit is high, your stance must still appeal vehemently to the people you are trying to persuade. After all, few people will jump on board a train that will bring them to ruin or even mild discomfort even if your mouth is sweet. Effective persuaders must be adept at describing their positions in terms that illuminate their advantages. As any parent can tell you, the fastest way to get a child to come along willingly on a trip to the grocery store is to point out that there are chocolates by the cash register. It is a process of identifying shared benefits and cannot be termed as deception. It is just a persuasive way of framing the benefits of taking such a journey.

TRUTH IS HARD! BUT SAY IT!

This world is not all a bed of roses; the same holds in marketing. Marketing isn't always about roses and rainbows. Sometimes, you have to be the bad cop in your marketing by telling people the hard stuff because honest confrontation is tough. No one wants to hear that the reason they are having a tough time is because of a factor dependent on them, but by making them aware that you are putting the ball in their corner.

Take, for instance, you are selling an exercise product or service such as a book, video, or class. You can tell people point blank that there is a solution to them with getting in shape, and the only reason they are not getting in shape right now is that they have not made the right decision yet to do so. The solution is right in front of them as to the efficiency of the package. All they have to do is take advantage of it.

Thus, when confronted with the inescapable facts of what they had said about themselves and what customers had told us, it is required of the marketing manager to say the truth. Once you have the truth, people need aspirational goals to cross that uncomfortable gap between the truth and the goal; you must set very achievable, step-by-step measures. The process of doing begets progress. Along the way, you must remind people of how far they've come already and how much closer they are to achieving the goal. That's when you see the light in their eyes. All these things, honest self-assessments, setting goals, and marching toward them-form a constant process, and they are also what makes managing fun and profitable.

It is unprofessional to profess your interpretation of what's wrong and beat people up; to motivate them to change, you must show them a mirror that would express your sense of transparency. Likewise, it is better to write down comments customers had said about us, both good and bad.

ASSERT AUTHORITY

The market is not about you but your customers; therefore, it should be focused mostly on your customers. When you talk about products or services, you shouldn't talk about features but benefits; customers are more obsessed with what benefits they could gain from your products than who you are. The only time you should make marketing about you is when you are at the stage of asserting your authority.

Whether you are selling a course, a book, or a service, you want to establish yourself as an authority in your market. What makes you the person to trust to deliver the product or service? If you're the most knowledgeable, then where did you get your training? If you're the most recommended, then who do you get your recommendations from? Simple!

Do well to use your authority through credible sources when possible; this is the part of your marketing where you drop specific names, certifications, experiences, celebrity endorsements, media spotlights, and testimonials from other recognised names in your industry, etc. Don't be shy or humble. Persuade your customers by making it known that you are the best person or business to turn to that can offer the best product or service.

PERSISTENCE PAYS!

Some people assimilate information once, some twice, while others take longer to accept a concept due to various factors specific to individuals. Marketing is not a onetime effort because someone doesn't consume your content or make a purchase; you can't give up on them. Persistence is persuasive.

At times, your potential customer is not ready to buy today. Maybe they won't be ready to buy whatever you're selling next week either. However, once they have seen lots of great information coming from you over the long haul, they may get to the point that they are ready.

The best way to keep track of their willingness is to make sure that you are there in their inbox, on their Facebook news feed, or in their *Google* search results when they are ready. If you are persistent in your outreach and promotional efforts, you might just be able to persuade them to choose your product or service when the time is right. It is that simple!

GET CELEBRITIES TO YOUR SIDE

Celebrities are public figures who can serve as role models for a large number of masses. Even though not everyone knows a celebrity, most people know a celebrity in their industry. If you don't have concrete proof for the things you are marketing or if you simply want to enhance your current marketing efforts, getting endorsements from celebrities and influential people, your industry will move forward.

Also, there are surefire ways you can use social influence on your e-commerce site, which includes reviews that help validate your claims. It is one thing for you to say, "This backpack is durable." It's more impactful when a customer says the same thing. These reviews can be accomplished by adding a review widget to your site for each product you offer.

However, it is not enough to add a widget; you have to be proactive about getting them. Once you add the widget, people get stuck on a decision, they look to see what other people do, and this is why a recommended product widget can help lift conversions. When people don't find what they want, they leave. Providing additional suggestions to them might persuade them to check out other products.

The foundation of this method is by looking through your e-mails, testimonials, recommendations, or other communications to see if any big names have given you their seal of approval in any way. If it's directly linked to your promotion, such as an endorsement for the product or service you are selling, that is perfect. If not, you can give free products to celebrities by reaching out and ask celebrities and Influential people to test out what you're selling and report back to you. This may also require that you pay them for their time and promotional efforts, or that you make them an affiliate partner, but it could yield significant increases in sales, eventually.

CONCLUSION

These persuasive skills are not the only ones that could be instrumental in getting massive sales for your products, packages or services; however, these are some of the easiest to explain and some of the most proven if combined prudently with the discussed elements of persuasive marketing. It is now the responsibility of a marketing manager, based on the wealth of knowledge and exposure, to find the ones that fit best with your business's goals, mission, products, and services. Then, start implementing them throughout your marketing strategy, both online and offline? This is almost the best of all materials that could make you effective in the sphere of persuasive marketing.

COMMUNICATION IN MARKETING

arketing communication refers to the medium that businesses use to deliver messages to consumers, directly or indirectly, about the goods and brands that they sell to persuade them to purchase.

In other words, the various means by which the organisation shares information with consumers about its products and services is called marketing contact.

The seller uses marketing strategies to build brand recognition among potential clients. This means they are building a picture of the brand in their minds, which helps them make a buying decision.

The seller uses marketing strategies to build brand recognition among potential clients. This means that a brand identity is developed in mind, which helps them decide on the purchase.

Marketing communication includes sharing context, knowledge, and ideas about the goods and services between the source and the receiver, and about the business that sells through promotional content through advertisement, advertising, sales management, and sales promotion.

The source in marketing is the seller who wants to publicise the product. The seller sends a message to a recipient who is part of the target market. Consumers interpret the message and incorporate it, and they continue to buy it when their investment is affordable. Feedback is the reverse flux of seller contact.

Marketing communication can be skewed, especially when a message goes through multiple channels. Noise is highly destructive. Incorrect shipping and receiving will bring about the noise. The loudest noise is competitive communication.

Marketing communication refers to a company's or individual's strategy of targeting its target audience through various forms of communication. Marketing communication involves ads, direct marketing, branding, packaging, distribution, appearances at the trade show, etc.

Communications marketing provides answers to the following questions:

- How should they use the product?
- How can one use the product?
- Who will use this product?
- Where can one use the product?
- When will they use the product?

Marketing communication includes advertising, sales promotion, sponsorship events and experiences, public relations, direct marketing, interactive marketing, word of mouth, and personal sales.

ELEMENTS OF MARKETING COMMUNICATION

ADVERTISING

The business uses an indirect and paid way to educate its customers through television, radio, print media, and online websites on their goods and services. Advertising is one of the most widely used means of communication, with precise detail on the goods of the organisation available and facilities readily available for communicating to the same target audience.

SALES PROMOTION

The promotion of sales requires a range of short-term consumer opportunities to buy products and services. Not only does this help to link existing customers, but this advertisement platform also attracts new consumers with added benefits. Sales promotion tools include Discounts, refunds, a one-to-one free purchasing programme, coupons, etc.

EVENTS AND EXPERIENCES

Different businesses plan activities, such as sport, entertainment, non-profits, or community events, to create a long-term link to their brand in the minds of consumers.

The name of the sponsor organisation is visible at playing fields, player uniforms, trophies, entertainment event rewards, after-School activities, etc.

PUBLIC RELATIONS AND PUBLICITY

Companies conduct various social events to create the right brand image on the market. Some of the traditional ways to boost public relations are performing activities such as constructing public buildings, donating part of their purchases for the upbringing of children, the organisation of blood shops, the planting of trees, etc.

INTERACTIVE MARKETING

Recently, interactive marketing has grown to be a marketing communications tool for customers to interact with online firms and solve their questions online.

Amazon is one of the best interactive marketing examples, in which customers have the choice and the order in the past.

WORD-OF-MOUTH MARKETING

It is one of the most widely used forms of communication by which consumers exchange information about the products and services they recently purchased with colleagues and friends. This is important to businesses because the brand identity depends on what the consumer thinks about the brand and the message he sends.

PERSONAL SELLING

This is the conventional marketing communication system, where sellers approach potential buyers directly and provide them with information about their products and services. This correspondence is considered one of the most trustworthy because it is verbal, that is, face-to-face, or written via e-mail or SMS.

MARKETING COMMUNICATION OBJECTIVES

Communication goals in marketing are long-term strategies in which marketing campaigns can add value over time to the brand. In comparison to sales promotion initiatives, which include short-term procurement incentives, and communication objectives are useful if you convince consumers that your brand provides the desired benefits always.

TO INCREASE AWARENESS

Enhanced brand recognition is not only one of marketing communications' most important goals. It's also the first one for a new company. You must tell customers that your business and its goods and services are present when you reach the market first.

These can include radio or newspaper advertisements reflecting the logo of your company and your brand name, slogans and jingles repeated continuously. The entire target is to be memorable and established.

Developed businesses also aim at building or sustaining an increased understanding of the closely related target. This means the consumers first think about you when they look at your product category.

TO CHANGE ATTITUDES

Another communication goal is to improve the image of a product or brand. Often your business, your goods, or your services in the market lead to misunderstandings.

Publicity is a way to answer them explicitly. In other instances, ads are harmful because the organisation is engaged in an incident of market controversy or concern.

TO INFLUENCE PURCHASE INTENT

An essential communication goal is to enable clients to buy. This is usually achieved by compelling ads, which gives the seller competitive advantages over rivals. The underlying requirement or desire that motivates a consumer to act is essential. It is important.

The use of sport drink advertisements to encourage buying intentions by athletes running, heating up and drinking, and sweat is a standard method. The ads usually include the flavour and nutrient benefits of the drink.

TO STIMULATE TRIAL PURCHASE

Two different communication objectives, which are intricately linked, are to promote research and facilitate repeat purchases. Free tests or product samples are common strategies to encourage consumers first to test their products. The goal is to reduce risk and bring your brand to life.

You will need to figure out how to turn it into an additional purchase when they first purchase it. Discounts on potential sales or frequency plans are ways to make frequent purchasers and loyal customers for unique users.

TO DRIVE BRAND SWITCHING

The promotion of rebranding is also intricately linked to the use of stimulating studies. This is a deliberate strategy to get clients who buy rivals goods to turn to their brands. Tidal detergents are used to inspire rebranding in contrast to "Other leading brands."

The downside of this is that consumers already shop within their range of items. This means that the necessity is remembered. You just have to convince them of the quality of your product or service and prove it.

PROCESS OF COMMUNICATION IN MARKETING

Marketing communication involves an exchange of meaning, information, and ideas between the supplier and buyer of goods and services, as well as the company that promotes through ads, advertising, sales marketing, and sales promotion through promotional material.

When it comes to ads, the seller who wants to promote the company is the source. The retailer delivers a message to a customer who is the focus community of buyers. The consumers interpret the message and implement it, and if their money is inexpensive, they want to buy it. Feedback is the opposite flux of seller touch.

Marketing communications can be distorted as a message is passing through several networks. Faulty transmission and reception can cause noise. The most extreme noise is aggressive contact.

Communication is a way to communicate both verbal and nonverbal messages. It is a continuing operation and a contact message is needed. This message will be transmitted over a channel to the recipient.

The receiver must recognise this message in terms that the sender provides. You have to answer within a specific time limit. Therefore, correspondence is a bidirectional and imperfect mechanism without input from the receiver to the sender.

THE MAIN COMPONENTS OF THE COMMUNICATION PROCESS

The context in which conversation takes place is affected by this. This may be a physical, psychological, statistical, or cultural context. All communication is conducted within context. In a context, the sender selects the message to communicate.

SENDER

Senders/encoders are individuals receiving a letter. A sender uses symbols to transmit the message and to produce the answer needed. The sender may be an entity, a group, or a body. The thoughts, history, concentration, expertise, competencies, and awareness of the sender have a significant effect on the post. The chosen verbal and non-verbal symbols are essential to decide the recipient's message interpretation in terms given by the sender.

MESSAGE

The letter is a crucial concept the sender wants to express. It is a signal that evokes a response from the receiver. The contact cycle begins with the decision about the letter to be sent. This needs to be assured that the message's principal purpose is obvious.

MEDIUM

The medium is a platform for message sharing/transmission. The sender must choose an appropriate medium for distributing the message, or the message may not be transmitted to the intended recipient.

The recipient must select an acceptable means of communication to understand the message accurately and correctly.

RECIPIENT

Recipients/decoders are people the message is meant for. The degree to which the decoder understands the message depends on multiple variables such as the understanding of the listener, their reaction to the message, and the encoder's reliance on the decoder.

FEEDBACK

Feedback is the critical component of the correspondence process, as it helps the sender to evaluate the message's effectiveness. It lets the sender ensure that the decoder is reading the message correctly. Feedback can be either verbal or nonverbal. This may also be in written form in the form of notes, surveys, etc.

GAINING CUSTOMER ATTENTION

As an entrepreneur or small business owner, you've already been in a position where one of your job's main activities is to attract more and more potential clients into your business. You always have to get the attention of the customer.

Moreover, if you do have customers, you need them. It can never suffice for your small company. It is for this purpose that the job is to draw constant customer attention.

While it seems easy, more work is needed in the process.

You have a company. You've got a product or service, and now you need people to listen, understand, and believe you are here to fix your bad, dull, and irritating consumer issues.

The first step is turning them on. While that doesn't ensure the company's success, it's the first step you need to take on the part as an entrepreneur.

You can take various steps or more than ten steps. Most notably, however, to draw more and more clients, you need something like your regular business routine.

Your business solves consumer issues and needs. You need to invest time in your everyday life to find prospective clients with issues or desires of this kind.

You can help them solve their problem if you encounter these clients or recommend one of their solutions. Because the topics are more complicated than anybody can think, when you give them a helpful way to fix their challenges, though, and see the business as one of the stops in that direction, they will gain their attention.

They must know that you are the right person for them if you want to draw customers to your company. The best way to show you are the right person for them is to demonstrate your experience consistently and share your experience with the crowd.

Social media is becoming one of today's most important market tools that can help you with such events.

Why not make a cold call and ask for free advice from two future customers? It is one of the most effective means of establishing high-quality ties with your future customers.

You can also send one weekly promotional e-mail advertising your products and services.

In this way, using useful suggestions, you build credibility and try to market and promote all of your goods and services in the same manner.

In your industry, there are likely to be many forums where you can build connections with helpful advice and answers to questions that are closest to your own experience.

Customer recommendations seeking to utilise your products and services are one of the most powerful marketing tools for small business owners. His usual method at work is to select one of his clients and ask them for feedback. Then you can quickly post those tips on multiple sites to build relationships on.

Psychology of Selling

In the world of trading, the most important thing to understand is that nothing happens until the sale is made. There are outstanding distribution departments, the most popular companies in the country. They go up or down if their promotional activities are of consistency. We should be proud to be vendors, and the whole country floats because of our efforts.

When we are adequately trained and certified in sales, there's no end on where we can go in this field. The 80-20 theory or the Pareto principle, prevails when it comes to sales. Twenty percent of retailers produce 80 percent of revenue, according to the 80-20 law. Once you're in the top 20 percent, you don't have to worry about money or work anymore. If you aim to reach the top 20 percent and the top 4 percent afterwards, you are one of the world's highest-paid individuals in the top 4 percent. The goal of *Psychology of Selling* is to teach you how to do this.

The competitive benefit hypothesis suggests the difference between people with excellent results, and those with average or poor results are not significant. There's always a little difference. Every day, the best employees do a little differently than other things. If you get this advantage, there's no reason why you can't get to the top 4 percent quickly. Selling is a game within itself. Which means what happens in the head of the retailer makes the difference in its success. We know there is a clear correlation between the self-image of a retailer and the efficiency and profitability of its sales. If we don't behave according to our description, we feel awkward. We will never receive any more or substantially less than our portrait. Our task is to increase your profit self-image.

We always sell in a way that is in keeping with our image. Some of us want to pick up the phone and contact someone. Some of us are feeling awkward at near. We feel more confident, we increase our self-image, and we are more effective. The root of self-comprehension is self-esteem — a human who loves himself with high self-esteem. How well you enjoy yourself in everything you do is essential to your success and effectiveness. Selling poses two significant barriers.

The first challenge is the assumption that the customer can make a mistake.

The second significant barrier to sales is the fear of rejection by buyers. As long as a seller does not build trust, a high degree of self-image, and adequate endurance to rebound from the eventual rejection, he cannot effectively sell out. All of the featured sellers have reached the point of not suffering rejection anymore.

Commonly, sales are based on friendship. People won't buy from you until they are truly sure you are their friend and act in their best interests. The link between your self-esteem and successful relationships with different people is clear. The hottest brands have the innate opportunity to make friends with prospective clients quickly. Enthusiasm is a crucial aspect of the business.

Selling is a movement of the love for the good or service into the other person's mind and heart. The reason so many people struggle in sales is that they don't last long enough to have the first positive opportunities that will improve their self-esteem and self-image and motivate them to have a good sales career. That's why it's so essential for you to say that nothing will stop you until you succeed.

DEVELOPING A POWERFUL SALES PERSONALITY

More essential than product awareness, selling skills, or the product is an excellent sales personality.

Top sellers have ten characteristics:

1. There is a high degree of autonomy and self-confidence.
2. The seller with high performance assumes full responsibility and sees himself as an independent.
3. The best seller's sales ambitions and desires are above average.
4. A high degree of empathy and consumer interest.
5. The salesperson who has success is highly focused on the target.
6. Your stamina is above average.
7. You should work hard and determined.
8. He trusts himself, his product, and his company.
9. Feature of the seller is that you and others are always absolutely honest.
10. Everywhere the best seller can make strange friends.

How do we achieve this profile and become a good seller? What are we doing? First, select the correct product. Some may sell objects, and some may sell incorporeal goods.

Then you must trust the product completely. Thirdly, your enthusiasm needs to be able to transfer your clients' thoughts. How are we strongly focused on the goal? Right and demanding targets should be accomplished. Set your goals for your activities to reach the desired level of income. There are a variety of appeals, follow-ups, collections, presentations, and so on. Once you set an aim, the plan is in the subconscious, helping you to meet your target quickly. Set goals for the individual and the family. Make a detailed list of all you want to achieve in sales.

Things tend to be going well when you feel good. The easiest way to put oneself in a good mood is to imagine. See you in your profession as the best. Take a look like you are making the most money. Wait every minute of the day to be assured. Professional salesmen have full confidence, are quiet, calm, and relaxed.

WHY PEOPLE BUY

It is essential to understand that people buy for their reasons, not ours. Every purchase decision is an attempt to improve because of that decision. The person who makes a purchase decision has three options: they can buy from you, from someone else, or nobody.

Every professional sale begins with a need analysis, and you can only sell once you understand what your product or service can do; then structure your presentation to meet those needs. Your job is to bring the person to a point where they focus entirely on how they can benefit from using your product, rather than how much they might lose if they commit to it. All purchasing decisions are emotional.

When we say we will do something for a logical reason, it means that we have invested more emotions in that reason than in any other. Every time a person says they want to think about it, they say that they have not caused their desire to own or enjoy the benefits of their product. The basic rule of sale is that people do not buy products; You buy benefits. Our job in the sales field is to figure out what benefits a person desires and would be willing to pay for it.

You discover needs by asking smart questions and listening carefully. If you let people talk for a while, they'll tell you about their basic needs or concerns about your product.

Naturally, people avoid new things. Build a product as something new instead of making it something new. Customers want a clear product or service reality. You want correct details about how your lives and business can be enhanced; they withstand high pressure and are upsetting. The key reason for the purchasing price is never rational and emotional for men. The quality problem should only occur when you compare your product to another product offered at a certain cost, and the individual should be concerned about quality for precise reasons. The sales presentation, the products, and the seller's presence reflect the quality of the product itself, depending on the viewpoint.

When a salesperson is well-clothed and polite, the business reflects an upscale reputation. Often, salespersons are the first engagement for a customer and can make or break your business. You will continue to sell efficiently, as long as you stay entirely focused on your clients and what they want and expect. Every sales presentation has a crucial advantage. The principal advantage that leads the consumer to buy the product is also one major problem -- the most significant challenge which prevents the person from purchasing the product. You discover the main advantages and the main problem during the sales interview. Many regard the quick access button as the most effective of all locks. The ability of the seller to decide the customer's principal reason for buying the product and then repeat it over and over again is crucial if quick access to the product is to close. Focus on the selling of this essential item.

CREATIVE SELLING

All best sellers are very creative. It's a matter of self-image. Most of us don't think we're particularly imaginative. We are not going to be if we believe we are not creative. We will continuously find new solutions if we think so. Specific questions, pressing tasks, and desired goals stimulate creativity. A profound understanding of your product or service will enable innovative sales. The better the product or service you are aware of, the more detail you master, the more creative you are in the transaction. The excellent seller identifies and focuses on a dedication to the best potential consumer markets.

One of the significant marketer's mistake they make is that they see all as equivalent when one prospect may often be a hundred times the value of another. We have to identify the best future for us. Ask yourself questions such as:

- Who is my customer?
- Who buys my product or service at the moment?

- In the future, who can afford it?
- In the past, who purchased it?
- Why do you purchase?
- Where can I benefit from my competitors?
- What should I offer nobody else?

Your principal task is to identify and build on these unique selling points, the competitive benefits that put you above all others.

Who's not your client? They're not people from you or your content; they 're not in the business. The most significant source of new customers is those who don't buy your product or another person.

Many people will not buy anything until they have somebody they respect to recommend it. That's why letters of testimony are so important. A report is worth an hour to reassure consumers that the product is excellent. The 20 ideas strategy represents an innovative way to double sales. Take your main issue and write it in a question on a piece of paper.

For instance, this year, how can I double my sales? How to increase the bid-to-call ratio? Then write the answers. You have many new ideas and ways to expand more company if you do it for two or three days so that you don't have time to do anything for the day. You will be one of the most creative salesmen and thus one of the most paying salespeople in your profession using this method.

APPROACHING THE PROSPECT

The cycle that ends with or not selling starts with the first interaction with the potential buyer. Every word must, therefore, be prepared in advance in your emphasis or introduction. The interest of the future customer will kill your strategy. You can never get to the foundation for a presentation if you don't crack this fear.

You only have 30 seconds to get the attention of the target at the beginning of the emphasis. Your opening question should also be planned, memorised, and regularly practised word by word. You must be comfortable with all. He wants to know five things before the prospect is relaxed and listened to you. You want to ensure that you are aware of something important, that you speak to the right customer, that your visit is short, that it's not binding, and you don't push it too much.

If scheduling an appointment on the phone, there are some factors you must consider. Ask your company for a well-structured and for an original query. Be compassionate, polite, and firm, but argue not. Make sure that you do not use high-pressure tactics; reiterate that your company is important to the customer. Do not speak by telephone or e-mail about your suggestion. Offer for your office to submit the details. Set an offensive and the consistent yet courteous date and time for an appointment. Smile and smile on the phone. Thank them for their time and repeat your appointment date and time.

Take a break before the sales call and visualize a simple, confident, cool, optimistic, happy image of yourself and the interview in full power. Always set up your show when you are standing. You risk devaluing your product if you don't. Someone looks at a valueless commodity when they are willing to sell it because they are in a showroom. They are willing. A calm, optimistic, and relaxed salesman's proposed impact is very high. The majority of skilled sellers relax us. You must always radiate trust in yourself and your company. Therefore, we have faith when we hear and see it. Their look, their voice, and their attitude are three significant influences. You create a commercial atmosphere if you look confident with a loud and clear voice, instead of quiet, shy or withdrawn, and your attitude is relaxed and optimistic. The best possible light should always be shown by your company. The proposed results of a safe, smooth, efficient, and desirable product affect people. Your environment should be sound and clean, and bring success and prosperity, especially if customers arrive at your office.

Our body language is important because 80 to 9 percent of our total communication is nonverbal. Stand up and sit down, sit straight. When talking with people, you never cross your arms, because that means you closed them off to further communication. Crossed legs, above the knee, indicates that you are withholding the information. Did you know that? You should lean slightly into your best spot. Look at the scene, listen, nod, and smile. Look carefully and listen intently. Please seek to reduce noise and sales damage. Always be respectful and courteous. Patients, friends, staff, and receptionists will be taken into account by your customer. One of the fundamental rules for sales is that everybody is treated as a one-million-dollar prospect or as a customer.

THE PSYCHOLOGY OF CLOSING

The closing part of a sales presentation is the most difficult. Closing is our job as a retailer, and the part which the consumer hates is too. We dedicate ourselves to running our customer's deal seamlessly and painlessly. Detail your title and make a sales presentation thereon. There are several key closure criteria. You have to be optimistic, motivated, and eager to finish sales. You must be mindful of the customer's requirements.

The customer needs to understand what they offer and the value of what they offer. You and the business need to trust the client. It must trust you, and a certain degree of relationship and friendship must exist. The customer needs to take advantage of the bid. The only pressure you have on a sales show is the silence pressure after the final question. Common buying signals must be recognised.

The customer can speak, rejoice, or ask for the price or delivery more quickly. Any change in attitudes, voices, or behaviour may mean that a decision to purchase is nearby. Once you look at the person's behaviour, ask a final question. "Are you ready to make the purchase?"

It can be difficult to graduate for several reasons. First of all, the inherent rejection apprehension of the seller. As the fear of consumer disappointment, fear of buying or charging too hard is another challenge. Never speak about your other clients or argue with him about your prospects. Don't offer your views on personal issues, faith, politics, unions, health, family, etc.

Make it clear that your competition can never beat your service or price. Always guarantee that you can't sell too much, or say that the company can do something that you can't -- negative biases, the fact that the individual does not purchase in advance, decrease their passion. Nothing will ruin sales more quickly than a lack of enthusiasm on your part. Very often we find that our customers and we have various wavelengths. Another employee of your company will call you instead of losing the customer to your company.

WINNING CLOSING TECHNIQUES – I

A series of questions leading up to or partial closure, each of which requires an affirmative answer. The questions start with the most general questions, then go to more specific questions. Though a person pays more closely to the consumer than they are interested in or able to purchase, it will be difficult to say "no" after that if you can ask six "yes" questions at the start of your presentation. Virtually all life insurance, trade products, educational products, mutual funds, brokerage, and banking services are on the increase.

It's especially important to complete the invitation. You must submit a direct or indirect purchase request at the end of your sales presentation. One of the most powerful is, "Why do you not attempt to do it?" When first mentioned, no one can pay the price. The justification is the rule of the omitted alternative. Since we only have a few sums of money, all other things we might buy with that money are removed by each transaction.

There are two different things; willingness to pay and ability to pay. The way to improve payment preparation is to increase the buying need. Don't talk about the price as long as you can avoid it. It always speaks of advantages. Price resistance is simply an opportunity to tell him that he did not provide you with enough proof that the benefits outweigh the price. Such suggestions will help you with price complaints. Discuss only the price at the customer's request. Concentrate always on their interest, not the money that you will earn as a result of the sale.

There are always good price explanations. Don't address value and profit at the same time without considering worth. Compare the price to the costliest items and extend the premium over the product's life. Many forms of money and demand issues are handled using processes. If a prospect says that they can't afford it because business is bad at the present, which is seldom the case, you must provide him a compelling reason to buy now and not put off the purchase. How about saying, "Right now you may have little money, but the price is likely to increase the more you wait." By saying this, it gives the buyer something to think about, which is saving money by purchasing the product now.

If a potential customer says that budget constraints do not permit purchases, then consider offering a postponement billing until the next budget period. If a customer says that they have not expected this to cost so much, reassure them that there is very good price justification and speak about its costs and drawbacks. If a customer hesitates to make a purchase at the end of the visit, keep offering information on how the purchased good will benefit them. Always remember, that everything that you say it about them and how their life will improve because of the purchase. Take the completed sales agreement and tell him this is a good thing.

WINNING CLOSING TECHNIQUES – II

Below you will find some of the most simple, common, and effective locking techniques ever created. The second assumption concerns a minor point in the sales submission, which means that the whole deal is approved. For instance, the person looks at the refrigerator and says, "I want it blue or green." The seller does not take this for granted and by you saying, "Would you like us to bring you this home this afternoon, or will it be all right tomorrow? " the deal is immensely powerful.

The person didn't say "yes" or "no." When someone hesitates, stop the presentation and say, "Oh, only a moment before our continuation, we 're going to make sure we can get it." If you have a detailed list, the summary is excellent in the end. Provide your customers with the advantages they can enjoy from the product and then place them on the list and plan on presenting them in the right order.

Pay attention to and repeat the one or two advantages that appear to be of most significant interest for them. Puppy products are valued in the billions of dollars. The aim is to let potential customers touch, test, feel, retain, or test the service or product. If you have a product that a person can try or take home, for example, use this option. Take a piece of paper and draw a line in the middle. You write on the one hand that the decision was made.

In comparison, the consumer writes arguments for this. The fulfilment of the order is another assumption. Once you arrive or talk with the prospective customer, please fill in and fill out an order or sales contract form or a form. After the conversation, a modification should be made to delete or finalise the contract or order form.

The end of the related story, since people like stories, is important. He tells a story about a satisfied customer who was as indecisive as the prospective customer, but he took his advice, bought, and was very satisfied with the product. If you have a recall policy, make sure you market this drug for years to loyal buyers and that most of them have ordered it from you before delivery. Today, only if you create a reason for making the customer an offer that is valid today or not tomorrow will you likely close the deal. Using launch approval, tell him that he will proceed, but you know that for the best price, he will return.

If the customer refuses to buy, the lost selling or closing of the door button is used. Tell the actual reason you haven't bought it when you wake up. If that is the explanation, go back and try to close again; a source of recommendations is any buyer or non-buyer. A 10-15 times cold call interest is moved. Once you have sold your recommendation, you should immediately call new stakeholders. You will greatly increase the efficiency of your sales calls by creating a framework for receiving and implementing the advice.

MANAGING YOUR TIME EFFECTIVELY

The sellers' time managed effectively is one of the most significant problems to achieve. It works only if you face an area, an outlook, or a client. It does not work if diagrams or recommendations are removed. Uncertainty and pause are the biggest waste of time along with postponement and interaction with strangers.

You waste your time, if you are unwilling to close, or if you are not asking for the sale often enough, so you must continue to focus on the outcome of closing the deal. Inaccuracies and shortcomings are a big waste of time. Make sure all the records are correctly completed and print them out in advance. Lack of product awareness in a geographical area is a waste of time, unsubstantiated appointments, and poor call preparation.

Time hassles are perfectionism or insistence that before being sold, distracted or wandered and fatigue or overwork; everything is in perfect order. A person lacking passion, motivation, and energy will achieve little. By using your resources to maximise efficiency, you will increase the effectiveness of your sales. Future planning is important; every day ahead of schedule. Go to bed early. You owe it to yourself. Every morning for 20-30 minutes, read the motivation or inspiration for your sales. Planning early every morning for your day is critical. Always have a plan and make a To-do list.

People with less time are almost always your most precious prospect. There are not enough people who do not do any business selling. Spend 75 percent of your time looking until you see customers who are distracted. Spend the entire day of your work focused on meaningful and productive tasks because every minute counts.

Think of your day in minutes and hours; don't think about getting finished with it or quitting early. Don't think morning and afternoon. Don't think morning or evening. In minutes, think about it. You can earn up to two and a half to three months of extra earnings every year if you make good use of your time and shave off minutes from your lunch and coffee breaks by finishing up a little earlier. Listen to motivational audio tapes in your car during these times as well as while driving to and from work. Consider cutting your television's cord and use that time for more productive means.

Enhance your sales skills continuously. Make the most of your time if you can increase the proportion of close lectures. Note that you only sell if you have a qualified person who can purchase.

MANIPULATION TECHNIQUES

I can make you believe in something that you don't believe in with modern retargeting. I'm saying that I can, I hope everybody can -- media, government, salespeople, owners of online companies.

You see, the mind mostly functions unconsciously. Every second of your surveillance day, vast amounts of information are recorded and leaked. Should that be the case? If I did not collect the information, spit it out, and make assumptions on the back, you would not survive the day. You don't get what is happening whether you browse through Facebook or check *YouTube*. You report it, though, or wonder if it's real, and often you don't understand the message. You are on the autopilot and build assumptions and expectations about it subconsciously.

Let us admit that in the consumer web industry, we are in the manipulation business. We create products that persuade people to do what they want. We call these people "users," and although we don't tell them out loud, secretly, we expect them to be detestably addicted to each other.

Our technologies are put to sleep by users. When they wake up, they look for reports, tweets, and updates to tell their loved ones, "Good morning." The famous game manufacturer and professor call the 'cigarette of this century' wave of habit-building technologies and call them addictive and potentially destructive.

Manipulation is the ability to change others' behaviour or perception, intelligently, or unscrupulously. The term has negative connotations for many people. The idea that marketing manipulation can be used evokes images of frightening tactics and deception.

It's not a bad thing though as marketing requires some coercion. Marketing manipulation is a useful tool from an ethical perspective to reinforce your brand. Tampering can impact your long-term market goals when performed improperly.

If you own a company, it's your job to manipulate marketing. Only thus do enthusiastic fans gain their confidence, sell them products. It's part of what you do to manipulate. The key is, therefore, not whether you do so, but how.

The best companies I know are mindful of how they use media manipulations. You don't, and you oughtn't to feel guilty. It can have a positive impact on your audience because it is done correctly.

For example, take Amazon. Have you ever found a book you love because it was recommended by Amazon when you looked for the author's website?

Google, how about it? Have you ever met an influential or thinker you love and follow because Facebook one day highlighted their message?

Well-finished, exploitation of the ads is fine, but it can quickly smell in the wrong hands, like most good things.
It begins with a deep understanding of your offer or product. Does it change? Is this a 'vitamin' or a 'pain alleviator?' Are you the real deal between you and you? Will it impact the other person really and massively? You must trust what you do and commit yourself to the best.

You must know who's helping once you do that. You must also be profoundly aware of your crowd. Right now, what's your main problem? What's your greatest pain? Avoid this pain and withstand the action?

It is, therefore, a good thing to manipulate marketing because it feels good in our DNA. It is to escape the dangerous circumstances that we have come to exist. Thus, we stay in our comfort zone and are blind to the necessary solutions.

MANIPULATION IN MARKETING

Nobody wants to be manipulated, but you can refer to a dictionary description if you're not sure whether it is. It is said that manipulation "handles or affects skillfully," which doesn't sound very bad. However, you can find another concept that seems to validate your most extreme fears. You should proceed to read. Manipulation is designed "to control or to play for its benefit by inventive, unfair or insidious means." You know that you should stop, but it's hard to say that it's a specific social influence that a writer and manipulator wants to change the way people perceive or conduct through abusive, disappointing, or abusive tactics.

You learn that deceit or misrepresentation is typical of abuse, and it is quite different from persuasion since there are unclear motives of coercion.

It's good to know it because a suspect vendor might one day attempt to darken his door by offering to invest in misleading advertising as a small business owner. These advertisements might make you believe twice like the salesperson who pushes designer jeans -- is it or isn't it tampering? Therefore, it is sensible for a group to take advice that even handles manipulative advertising so seriously.

Your mind navigates the surrounding day with an unconscious knowledge of the world. In the world today, there is a lot of information. Your mind should absorb, filter, and process assumptions for decision-making. That is why the unconscious mind forms beliefs and assumptions on much of what you see.

This fact is extremely important in marketing. Both mainstream and new media, major brands build ubiquity. You want to preserve your connection with your goods. If the advice is right, companies will attract their customers over their lives and evolve for themselves.

Manipulation was often a marketing feature. Now, however, more than ever is at stake. With the commonly available algorithms on search engines and e-commerce websites, they can be ready to manage the order or updated.

The seller has a chance to manipulate his audience by choosing his brand, understanding it, and make use of targeting. These ideas can assist consumers in purchasing your product or service. Fortunately, you can manipulate them also ethically and fairly, not through disappointment.

ETHICAL MANIPULATION

Manipulation of marketing is just a part of the equation, no matter how you execute the plan. It's not about integrating manipulations into the approach, nor how they're taken into consideration.

Regardless of how you feel about coercion, this is just part of the message that you have to consider. There's no need to feel bad or that you betray someone because ethical manipulations have the potential to affect your audience positively and change your customers' lives.

You've already seen ethical exploitation as a customer. If you have ever been influenced by a campaign you've noticed, found new items you wanted, or encountered new leaders of opinion on social media, that was the result of targeted manipulation and acts.

HOW TO USE MANIPULATION IN MARKETING ETHICALLY

The effective and ethical application of deception starts with the analysis of your product or service from inside and to your customers. You have to ask, "What does the product or service provide? How it helps and how it impacts." There are other questions that bring you closer to your customers' thinking.

And like your customers, you must also remember to ask questions such as, "Who are you here? Who are you? What are you doing? What are you doing? Will it take to fix any problems? What are the big flaws? Does it always have to be sensibly addressed?"

You can thus learn a little more and what you can offer your customers. Not only does it help you reach the right audience with the right message, but it also gives you pride, passion, and commitment to the product or service you offer.

You may also have to make your weaknesses and problems known to them and seek the solution you offer. They guide you through the process and give you the tools you need to solve your problems.

THE ETHICAL WAY TO APPROACH MANIPULATION

A small amount of manipulation is necessary to help your audience, but there is a way to help your clients. An overview of some ethical methods is provided below.

- **Keep it relevant.** Without too much substance, don't include overly sales-related detail. Give your clients additional value, which provides more than just what you can do for them.

- **Working for omnipresence.** The way your customers are brought to your solution is not fast. You will also still strive to keep up. Your business is the one that was there as soon as anything clicks.

- **Gain trust and preserve it.** Each interaction with your audience should add value and simultaneously demonstrate the genuineness of your brand. This will increase your trust and solve your difficulties along the way.

When you follow these principles, the marketing strategy is legal before the consumer takes the steps it needs. Old-fashioned marketing tactics used to rely on insecurity, frightening tactics, cheating, or assault for the job. This approach does not serve your customers well, however, and will only reduce their trust over time.

TIPS FOR ETHICAL MARKETING MANIPULATION

There are many ways to attract and retain customers in an ethical, legal, and respectful manner by manipulation and consumer psychology. Here are some tips to add an ethical way to the strategy and message of your campaign:

- The consumer's emotional and psychological appeals are more relevant than a product. It is so easy to preserve the emotions of your campaign that you focus on your product's advantages to your consumers and on how it will enhance their lives rather than promoting your product's characteristics.

- Consumers are sceptical more than ever before. You may doubt marketing claims more frequently. Do you want to have your marketing message trusted by your clients? Don't worry about exposing any of your mistakes and keeping your message clear and genuine.

- It is important that your brand is in the perfect position for your customers as well as being everywhere. You will try to put your rivals back in the mind of the customer. If the consumer finds a question and needs to be the first choice in the competition, then you want your brand to appear immediately.

- Exclusiveness is all because most people want to feel something special and important. This is more than simply saying that when your customers contact you, they have something special. Something essential must be secured.

- Use fear, question, or insecurity, but do not use frightening tactics. Stop using the spectacular claims of threatening and frightening your customers. Concentrate on how the clients can avoid worrying about their choices and make the improvements they need to fix their problems.

CONCLUSION

In principle, manipulation is a type of social action that should influence behavioural perception. It is a different story if this is done through dishonesty, frustration, or with violent strategies. Only with time will this tactic undermine a brand image. Also, although these tactics are widespread to consumers, there is little proof that they produce action.

Marketing deception based on consumer loyalty can be a successful technique for long-term economic growth and market success without frustration or coercive tactics. Companies can exploit their audiences and offer exceptional value to consumers by taking into consideration the needs and desires of customers, building trusting relationships, and evaluating long- and short-term motives and their effect on their clients.

GETTING TO KNOW YOUR BUYER

In this world where Smart + Connected is becoming a new daily life, it is our job to consider how people, our customers and users perceive emerging technologies, and how these technologies affect their daily life experiences. We are fully accredited chief technicians and human resources experts, as well as cultural anthropologists. The Intel staff and collaborators rely on clients and ecosystems: can we? We are asking: do we?

What's going to be the future experience? How can we build an ordinary future that allows all of us in the physical and digital world? We spend our days gathering extensive background information and analyzing how people live and work. The same data used to create people and other artefacts for the creation of experiences.

Within non-traditional environments (e.g., urban spaces), we also extend our research expertise and are responsible for pushing progress beyond the scope of current consumer study.

Your marketing message becomes more evident when you concentrate on the customer of your dreams, and your copy becomes sharp as the tip of a spear that cuts through the noise and eventually leads to a more profitable business. If you know the right people, it is crucial to have buyers of your dreams who benefit most and who pay the most for your products and services.

To develop products they will buy, we all need to know our consumers. That's how strong the notion of an audience that is minimally viable is.

It is not about your product but your customer. This means that you can gain a following through the internet, the occasional show, frequent restaurants, and months' downloads. You will hear about your needs and dreams, your goals, and your fears as this community expands.

Best way to define your potential buyer is having in mind the following:

1. Where does your dream buyer hang out and congregate?

Name the places where your dream buyers hang out and hang out online and offline, the better, the more informative, and the more specific.

"Hangs on Facebook," is too generic, while "Hangs on Facebook's Money-Making Machine," is more precise and successful.

"I like nature" is too generic to be insightful and feasible, while "I like going to the park every Saturday morning with your two children" reveals habits and values and is descriptive.

"Reading forums" is not targeted enough, but it is transparent and informative to "Reading obsessively from Reddit or HubSpot."

Understanding exactly where your dream customers are going can impact when to advertise, what to advertise, the sound of your text, and the slang language you can use.

2.   Where does your dream buyer get their information?

If your dream buyer is in research mode, where are they going to look for answers? Are they *Google*? One blog in particular? Reserves? Journals? *Youtube*? Write down your results in a simple phrase: "If Sally is curious about a subject, a *Google* search on her iPhone is the first place she goes."

3.   What are their biggest frustrations and challenges?

True understanding and empathy are essential to identifying your ideal buyer's avatar for your greatest problems and challenges. Knowing what it's like to be in your customers' shoes will help you create better products and services that answer your unique challenges and weaknesses.

Your ideal buyer's worries and problems are an important part of the products and services that you deliver. Whatever you sell has to solve a problem that is big enough for your dream buyer to happily part with your hard-earned money to solve it for him.

"When you imagine what the everyday life of your ideal customer looks like, you'll broaden your marketing with a personal dimension."

You can decide the feelings from which you talk in your copy and commercial when you learn your greatest problems and challenges. The emotions behind your dream buyer experience challenges, and frustrations can be sadness, anger, fear, regret, hope, and the desire for something better. When you are thinking about exactly what your dream buyer thinks, you will communicate with him emotionally on more than one reasonable level.

These will also mirror the kinds of stories you tell. In this case, the logic is simple. If a customer who has solved their greatest frustrations and challenges with your product or service sees a testimony from the buyer of their dreams, they are more likely to buy from you. You can see this positive change happens in a different individual.

4. What are their hopes, dreams, and desires?

When you know the buyer's expectations, aspirations, and desires of your aspirations, by using your goods and services, you will get a good picture of what life will be like. Imagine the vision being sold and an image of the promised land being drawn.

When your product or service makes the customer of your dreams understand your expectations, desires, and wishes, writing a copy for your landing pages, blogs, advertisements, and other tools that you used to sell more products and services would be much easier.

5.   What are their biggest fears?

What are the greatest fears of your dream buyer? What is it that keeps you awake at night? Who are they concerned about, but don't tell anyone else? A full understanding of your market's deepest and most basic fears is an aspect that is often ignored when designing a client's avatar. In my opinion, however, it is just as critical, if not more critical, than knowing your hopes, dreams, and desires. Why? For what? People are more inspired by pain than pleasure. They are more motivated by fear of loss than by a desire to win. Expressing the worries in the copies and ads is, therefore, an enormously important factor for getting your dream buyer to take action.

The strategy taken by insurance companies is a perfect example of the uncertainty that motivates people to act. Other than the advantages of advertising, you share the deepest fears of your future customers.

6.   What is their preferred form of communication?

E-mail? Chat? Live on Facebook? But do you want traditional postal services? It is a question of when the audience would like you to reach them. There, the simple lesson is to interact with your clients where they already are. Don't seek to push them to a more suitable location for you than where they are.

7.   What phrases and vernacular do they use?

Join the discussion already happening in the mind of the customer.

You see, in your customers' minds, these vocabulary and niche words are already being used for their hopes, dreams, pains, fears, and desires. Your job is to listen and write down on them. What industrial jargon do they use, and which specific and indigenous words do they use?

You need to record the exact terms and phrases they use and save them in a table to generate ideas for copies of blogs, landing pages, and advertisements and figure out where the buyers come together. Take those comments from Twitter, Facebook groups, or *YouTube* and record the audience's word-for-word responses. Today, scepticism is generalized. People are more attracted to people and companies who speak their language, have a sense of humour, or hold the same view than ever before. Each time you read your copy, your goal is to tell the buyer of your dreams, "Wow, it's like talking directly to me."

8.   What does a day in your dream buyer's life look like?

If you imagine what the everyday life of your ideal customer looks like, you will be extending your marketing with a personal dimension. It's convenient too. When's the right time to contact potential customers? What would you be most likely to answer? When are you most vigilant? Your dream buyer is completely different on Monday at 8:00 a.m. than on Friday at 6.30 p.m. Remember, use it in your marketing.

9.   What makes them happy?

It is more than an exchange of money for goods or services that customers travel. Your clients are emotional people who want to connect to make them feel good.

What contact points are you able to put on surprises, do random things, be amazing, and smile on your face during the journey of your dream buyer?

It may be a handwritten letter, a personalized birthday e-mail, or a free box full of company cookies. Who does not like cookies? After subscribing to this service, it may be thanks to you.

Inserting joy in the experience of the customer will create an emotional bond that encourages long-standing loyal fans and delusions.

Write a paragraph that summarizes your performance after answering all these questions. The effect is a much better understanding of when and how to meet and talk to the dream buyers. The results will lead to huge breakthroughs that will geometrically increase your business and allow you to dominate your market.

Defining your target market is one of the toughest things to do when you start a company. The good news is that once you do it, all crash rapidly. You just need to know what means can be used to achieve them effectively and what marketing strategies are the answers.

TIPS ON FINDING NICHE MARKETS HUNGRY FOR YOUR WORK

FIND A HUNGRY NICHE MARKET

The world is packed with creative advice. The purists of passions claim that all that you need to do is to find and to buy the right people. Business lovers claim that the balance between what is generated and what is compensated for by others has to be sought. Then we have the tough salesman who tells you to find a hungry market and then meet your needs, and soon!

As a creator of content, my opinion is that what I like to produce converges with what is required by the market. So when demand grows, and I can see that demand overlaps with my job, I can meet it.

SEARCH & OBSERVE YOUR CUSTOMER'S HABITAT

Mass marketing stopped and gave way to tribal groups with common niche desires, as the marketing guru once said. When the internet removes geographical boundaries, international web communities belonging to niches are found. The smaller the niche, the more enthusiastic the fan base.

I acted as a safari hunter and studied the actions and the world of my objectives -- science fiction and fans of fantasy, who like to play roles, too. On Twitter and blogs, I find some. In general, thousands of readers posted game-related tips, new findings in the novel, and the corresponding screenshots in public Facebook groups. For 2-3 months, I participated and helped answer questions and share tips in these Facebook groups. It was easy as it was an exciting sport. Hundreds of them posted and bought my latest book in the first 48 hours after I interacted with people.

Lesson: Find online groups and participate in them months before the product launch.

Lesson: People know you take your work seriously; you want to be supportive and know-how.

BE BEGINNER-FRIENDLY

It is recommended that you deliver as appealing and start-up-friendly as possible when you are new to a certain market, and people don't yet understand you or your goods. Enthusiastic audiences sometimes attempt new things in small niches, but I want to learn them in half as a content creator. That is why, to encourage readers to buy my new book, I took these precautions.

During the starting week, I gave many free digital copies and encouraged honest feedback. This is risk free because money does not have to be exchanged, and they can stop halfway if readers don't like your work.

I wrote a book that shows parallels to another popular series. Never equate your work to another one, but I think that it is rarely available to luxury beginners. This lets you compete with other jobs in the niches when you sell your latest unknown product, giving future customers a simple idea. You can drop this "crutch" marketing once you have developed yourself.

I began to test out new readers at a low price of $2,99. As prices are lower, a new reader has less investment risk. The .99 cent book could have been priced or distributed free of charge, but my staff told me this encourages readers to take and leave it on their Kindles or smartphones as dust collectors.

Lesson: As a beginner, the barriers that separate you from your customer are as many removed as possible. You can do this through gifts, reduced prices, and clear writing, which shows exactly what to expect from your prospects. Note: The customer doesn't purchase confused.

SELLING TO AN OVERCROWDED MARKET

The internet has helped us meet millions of customers, but there has been much concern that in a crowded market, how can you sell a digital product?

Whether you are selling e-books, pieces of training, or marketing content, your niche has competition, some of whom are better than you. A ton, a lot better. What must be done, then? Offline sobbing, calmly? No, not that.

PEOPLE ARE ADDICTED TO NEW THINGS

As you can see, every year there are tens of thousands of new books on the market. Will they have a need? All you have to do theoretically is read a few and be ready for life if you obey their suggestions.

There have been, and have been for decades, books on positive thinking, living in the moment, self-discipline, efficiency, habit growth, etc. Heck, the bestseller of over 3 million books called "The Power of the Now," although it simply responded to what the Buddha said thousands of years before.

Research has shown that people are drawn to and better treated by the news. Do not fear the abundance of products already available if you want to serve a hungry market. Research them and learn from them and understand how to differentiate.

SAME BUT DIFFERENT

People often say something completely different is something they like, but this is only partly true. The new job likes, but not if it is completely different, hungry customers have a certain expectation of your new product, and they shy away from you or scream worse if you don't deliver.

Seth Godin once clarified it beautifully; people are likely to become confused when you create a product outside the box. We are unable to position a product, and they rarely purchase frustrated consumers. On the other hand, you can create another commodity for me, which is hard to distinguish from the competition if you think in the shell.

The goal is to contemplate the box's edges. Comprehend the rules and smash them where best it seems.

This is the genre, and fiction means understanding the genre's tropics and then adjusting, some of them, to give the story a new perspective.

So when I write and publish my science fiction novels, I make sure I understand the following:

A) the genre conventions so I can satisfy the base of science fiction readers, and

B) separate the story from the competition enough. And it's getting out of place.

You need to find the right balance between satisfying your market expectations and taking a new turn.

LIKABILITY IS A DISTORTION FIELD; MAKE IT WORK IN YOUR FAVOUR.

When people know and like an artist, they seem to like and share the work more (art). My friend admitted not being the world's best illustrator, but her networking skills helped her to reach a vast number of potential customers. When some of her clients were asked why they chose her, they said they liked her, and they wanted to work with her.

It was not just his art; that was the reason.

Your service and product must be successful, but that alone does not guarantee sales. Creating real connections with like-minded people will give the goods a better look than they are. This is a big benefit in an online environment with competitive markets, which can make a difference.

How to annihilate competitors and

make more sales

It is also crucial that you know what your rivals are doing, but it is up to you to be creative and special. You must be the first to create a marketing plan. Only be yourself and be the first! If you always focus on your competitors, all the time they take away from your customers wasted, angry, and angry, it's time to attract more of your customers.

Get out of the crowd. Another one will sell similar products and services. Welcome to a prosperous economy. One thing that makes you unique forever as a small business owner is ... You! You! No-one will duplicate you and what you are getting. If replicating is easy, then it is time to stop being a victim. Dust those knees off and get back to the drawing board-concentrate the distribution, processes, and marketing activities to demonstrate the exclusive customer experience it provides.

If you are facing competition from a larger company, note that there is something extraordinary and marketable about small business: a personal touch, creativity, business principles, inventions... Using it to your advantage.

You've got to sell more than the competitors want. It's time to review your marketing plan because your customers are leaving your company en masse. There is a reason they are heading for.

It is time to be hungry and sit back on the bed. Identify what the customers don't want. Look at all aspects of your business: location, goods, employees, brand, etc. Call and ask why they have left your company. Using this market research to realign the processes (branding, marketing, advertising, communication, customer support, compliance) based on consumer expectations and not competitor activities.

Concentrate your energy on identifying your ideal customer. Then develop and execute a plan to earn your share of this niche. By winning customers who need and appreciate your services, you secure your market share despite the competition.

Let your competitors waste their time and money on marketing campaigns that are aimed at everyone. You will burn yourself or at least have wasted a lot of money. Your job is to offer your service or product to the perfect person for the right reasons at the right time. Dive deep into your niche and focus on marketing that is based on your needs and only your needs.

HOW TO STEAL FROM YOUR COMPETITOR AND GENERATE MORE SALES

If you want to increase your revenue and develop your marketing plan, your competitor's website will first test how to promote and distribute marketing material to your competitors.

When you are looking for help from your rivals, you will get a head start in your business. Learn from your mistakes, gain insight by tracking feedback from your customers, and even "steal" your strategic strategies.

Most companies don't find using their rivalry to their benefit. Why? Because of their biggest challenge is the rival, they kill themselves by not using what lies ahead-certain marketing tactics in the industry. Also, they are your greatest rival. Don't ignore the competition altogether. Most startups are not losing out on the competition, but because they are losing the will to fight.

Do not consider your competition an enemy but a motivation.

MONITOR WHAT THEIR CUSTOMERS ARE SAYING

Well, they're not going to skyrocket your conversions, but they've done you a lot of hard work.

To monitor customer reviews of a competitor's product is the best way to know what customers are looking to purchase.

Reviews are the perfect way to gain "secret" information about the product or service of your competitor. You'll see trends in reviews as you read them, trends you can use to build a counterstrategy to your company.

The higher the conversion rates, the more visitors you get to your website who are pleased with your bid. When you figure out which of the consumers of your rivals enjoy (or dislike) the product they bought or the interaction with their rival, they will immediately have the benefit. To make these dissatisfied customers your customers by meeting their needs and providing a product which makes them happy, you can market your product and brand.

Updating notifications or mentions of your competitor's products on social media could take a long time. Luckily, search flow fields such as Hootsuite track all of the companies that you want to pursue. By keeping an eye on consumer engagement with a rival, you will recognize the void that needs to fill your product or service.

The best way to check these tactics on your website is to break the calls to action and create valuable magnets (newsletters, e-books, white papers, etc.) after you have collected knowledge from the competitor's feedback.

SHOP THEIR MARKETING

"Imitation is the best flattery form," and the best way to learn from the competition.

Scan marketing messages from your rival to find out what appeals to them. Discover how to create trust and loyalty and who the consumers are. There is a good chance that your clients and your target group will be on an equal footing. If you figure out what's working for them, it could work for you too!

Were you too busy at tracking marketing messages from your competitors? There's a demand for that! Well, not exactly, but you can let *Google* do the job on your behalf.

Google Notifications is a perfect way to track the forum, expert community posts, or even their latest developments and connections for your competitor. *Google* Alerts can use social media or industry blogs to track competing companies. It is an easy way to remain up to date without keeping track of the websites of your business all day!

You can also allow marketing messages to reach you without the need to look for anything! Since the internet is so important to the business and the rise of digital marketing, there is a good chance that your competitor will have some sort of e-mail subscription to which he can subscribe. If your marketing material goes straight to your e-mail inbox, you'll be able to find successful tactics that you can incorporate.

This can also help you identify weaknesses that the industry can exploit. These vulnerabilities may create opportunities for you or indicate gaps in the business plan of your competitor.

If you are just starting the development of a marketing strategy, look at the big corporations. Even if they are not relevant to your industry, there's still a lot to learn. Successful companies such as Amazon, have developed their sales funnels and can model yours based on what works. Strategically position feedback, ratings, and related products to provide the best customer experience possible. Check the funnel functions to ensure it works for you before finalizing your strategy.

Modelling the sales funnel or marketing messages for a big company or rival will make a big difference in how website visitors are turned into customers. This does not mean copying your rival. Find strategies that you can implement to boost your company in your current strategy.

A word to the wise -- just because a marketing strategy works for your competitor, doesn't mean it will work for you. On your competitor's website, you may see a very brisk sales funnel, but there is no guarantee that it will work for them at all! Seek an A/B approach just to make sure that you are using the right one for you.

So don't copy your competitors, imitate their ideas and form your own!

STEAL THEIR LOST LEADS BY AVOIDING THEIR MISTAKES

As almost everything is digital today, your competitor can no longer hide behind carefully built brand identities.
You will assess where your competitor has lost the market by tracking feedback and searching digitally, and how your market will rush to save the day.

Maybe you will meet a dead horse, but I can't stress how important it is to read the reviews of your competitors -- mug reviews about what they do, right and wrong. If you research them, you'll be able to react to the worries, concerns, and suspicions of your customers before they occur, and how to make them your customers taking them away from your competitors.

There are some subtle elements you may not have thought about when scanning your marketing material on your website. They can also be very helpful in pointing out bugs from your competition that you can know and use on your website for ideas:

- **Approval seal:** Where do your confidence symbols come from? Do you have credible website approval? (Example: the angles list, Better Business Bureau, industry awards, etc.).
- **Social justification:** Are your social platforms embellished with customers' praise? How do you inspire your customers with your products?
- **Shape fields:** You have more or fewer fields than you? Type fields: Test A/B to find out what works best for you by testing more or fewer fields.
- **Price packages:** What techniques on your price page are you using?

You know where to improve your game when one of them is missing. Get reviews from satisfied customers and mark it on your homepage or develop a more user-friendly type for potential customers. You can adjust and help your company grow, which distinguishes you from your competition.

COMPETITORS CAN HELP YOUR BUSINESS GROW

This is almost a given, but it is possible to "steal" marketing tactics from your competitor to grow your business. They support not only your marketing messages but also help your company to grow internally by creating opportunities for increasing conversion levels.

Competition is good for every organization as it leads to self-confidence growth and the prevention of complacency.

Think about it. As an individual, your relationships can help you to grow. So why should the connection between you and your company be different?

You can create unique and creative viewpoints that attract prospective customers by increasing self-confidence, which also prevents you from being satisfied with an average product. Your competition keeps you current and innovative. It can also be a great way to measure your potential growth by measuring your growth. It will help you learn more about the competition and whether the market has matured. In any event, if you know that, you can grow. It may even help to narrow your niche in the industry and give your rival a competitive edge.

There's a possibility of dramatic changes in a mature market. Your product or service may be strategically positioned to completely disrupt the somewhat competitive market and draw the public's interest. If the market develops further, you will be asked to make your brand the best in your industry and to become the gold standard.

Competitive relationships are an intelligent business move, especially as you expand, and in any industry, you wish to become a household name. You will find out where your product is on the market and how you can put yourself best in your business by learning from marketing campaigns from your rivals. Similar tactics can be helpful in your marketing campaign, particularly if you just begin to have a vantage point!

Recall that competitors are friends, not enemies!

PERSUASIVE COPYWRITING

People have formed sentiments to increase the significance and, thus, our chances of survival of a particular, dangerous occurrence, for example. For example, if you are chased by a bear, you could run faster if you are scared and rationally knew, "This bear is going to eat me." The meaning of different events and options is constantly assessed by people. Our emotions and feelings are crucial to making sure the decisions we make are right for us and work for ourselves. Naturally, we can influence the gap in this crucial system of survival. Here, persuasive copying can shape the reader's perspective and influence buying options that are good.

Is it a sort of control of the mind? Not at all. As a neuroscientist, I, too, admire man's nature to assume that it can be driven as a shopping cart. However, you can unlock those drives and motives that the mind holder may not know with the right words or the right stories. We, humans, value better or positive information and ignore uncomfortably things we don't want to listen to, and that pleases us.

This means that when the reader makes a decision, it will read a rosy picture of life more enthusiastically than the one drawing attention to the possible disadvantage. No copywriter would do the latter, of course. However, social media reviewers or shoppers sometimes could find out what our real feelings are.

Copywriting used to be a term that was easy to describe. It was the text you found in news releases, direct mail, brochures, posters, and catalogues, and you saw or heard in ads on radio and television. Words sold out. There are other definitions -- some circulars, writing is editor-in-chief, something useful; the wording is any script designed to yield a result; conceptual thing, writing ads is a change in behaviour.

I think none of them cover the variety of platforms, methods, and contemporary writing purposes. How should we identify an activity that involves the process of attracting software bots ("bots") algorithmically managed to ensure a high-score website in a search engine? Creating blogging and social media-related relationships? Write webinar and video scripts in the app?

The sale can take time, of course, so do use the written word in newsletters, e-mail marketing, and on landing pages. To arrive at a workable description, we need to avoid thinking hard about the variety of networks and media that we have opened today, the sort of people who trade, more of them in a moment, and the narrow ones. Instead, we must concentrate on the underlying benefit that only text writing offers.

Copywriting is the practice of creating productive relationships with the written word, maintaining them, and expanding upon them to create a masterful image.

KNOWING YOUR COPY READER

You have to look inside their head and heart. What makes them drive? What keeps you motivated? What's turning you on? These are the stuff that you should be aware of before you start writing. Your customer comprehension should make it easier for you to sell them.

How could they be wrong? This is a letter from a commercial banking head, who presents its customer newsletter's winter edition. Therefore the purpose of the letter, the whole campaign, is to establish a good relationship with your business clients. Is that a problem with the training? The author doesn't know anything about combining mails. They probably don't care to think of it. Rather than feeling, "This bank knows me and looks after me," I felt "more bulk waste."

If I had not been a professional copywriter, I would have thought, "What's working for your reader?" Even as novelists need to understand their characters' inner workings, so do commercial authors must understand their readers. If we want the chance to get their attention and get the response we are looking for, we need to be able to remember your thoughts, likes and dislikes, hopes, and fears. We must remember that these are not data from a mailing list or demographic segment.

As a copywriter, sellers are among your most considerable resources. Unlike those of us who spend most of our time locked to a desk, sellers (or, anyway, decent people) spend most of their time in front of customers. Sellers know what's attracting customers to work. Buy a beer from them, and they can even tell you, and if you're a vendor, buy a beer for yourself! Well, that may sound impractical or sluggish. You may not have salespeople, or all of your clients do business online with you. Have you ever heard of the chat rooms? The more readers you meet, the easier it will be for you to publish. If you cannot find the answers, you will need to use a different tool in the toolkit of the author.

The closer you are to understanding as a human, the more qualities you will describe for your reader, with the related feelings "away from" and "toward." You create a feeling for him when you create a mental image of your reader, and what you have to say to make him do, think or feel what he wants. You have all kinds of information about them, of course, right? This can help you focus. Knowing the history of your purchases is not as important as knowing what type of person you are.

UNDERSTANDING WHAT YOU ARE SELLING

As we sit down to make a copy of the sale, most of us think about what we're selling. All too often, we rely on what the product is and not what it does. This is perfectly natural. After all, you tend to think a lot about copiers when you work for a copier manufacturer. When working for a retailer of designer glasses, you often think of designer glasses. The problem is that this is not an effective way to write. Although it may be the road to concise writing, product reviews seldom sell out. When you include the production workers in writing copies of the sales, you must be very patient. We are so in love with this idea we can't see any more. Tell a copier manufacturer what he does, and he'll tell you to "design a copier."

You have to know as a retailer that you are producing labour-saving equipment. The situation with designer glasses is close. These don't help people see better than regular glasses; this is about glasses that make a statement. Yet they are making people feel better than regular glasses. Your customer has no interest in your product. They think about what it's going to do for them. Saving you time? Saving money? Do you look good? Do you look winning? Become rich? If you're familiar with that, it should be. Let's get back to word B. You do know the advantages. It's an excellent position to know all the facts about your product, but you need to DRAMATIZE them in terms of profit to complete the sale.

The sales trainer has an old saying, "Sell, don't count." I talked about that in this section. It means that we focus on the benefits, not the features. There is, however, a variant of this sentence that works for us as copywriters even better. It is the "show, not count." We want our readers to paint a picture without it on living with our company and personality.

The picture of "life without a product" is necessarily darker. We imply negative consequences, a grim future. Even if it's all done with a gentle touch, you don't want your reader to despair.

These questions can be used to find routes in the minds of your reader, and the news that works best for you. Don't let yourself be distracted by apparent ambiguity. You have to work through them regularly and although each pair appears to be a mirror image of the other, the different connotations of "will happen" and "will not happen" contribute to subtle but essential discrepancies in the responses. Often your answers will also give you real sales levels.

WRITE LIKE AN ANGEL AND SELL LIKE A DEMON

Writing words and using formats to which almost all recipients react with indifference, apathy, or utter animosity immediately, makes a difference in the outcome. We strive to improve their way of thinking, feeling, and behaving. We ordinarily ask them to spend money. If that weren't hard enough, it's going to get worse. Since most of us were taught wrong-spelling, our professors, tutors, mentors, and administrators have insisted that we stick to the truth throughout higher education and in our professional lives. Nothing better convinces than the unrelenting accumulation of evidence. If you make the logical case strong enough, your reader will not be able to do more than comply. Even the most cursory look at our efforts so far, however, would indicate this strategy is far from fact. How many times do you feel like shouting, "What do you mean you don't agree with me?" Their points were impregnable, impeccable reasoning, and a robust plan. Something was lacking here and that was more of a feeling. I still believe that thoughts and feelings play a significant part in making decisions.

A strong copy doesn't have to be "elegant." However, there is a strong demand for the copy that creates trust, authority, relationships, and makes people chat, share, and buy.

It's possible to lack style, and writers who master this "style" are sought out and admired.

One of these writers was the legendary publicist David Ogilvy, who said, "Better advertising is one that sells the product without attracting publicity."

This doesn't sound intuitive, but it puts emphasis on it, and I'll explain why effective content marketing is based on this idea. Clear communication is the key to proper copying. Your best copy will be a "direct view window" and be present with your Windex every morning to make sure you're not distracting your clients and consumers from the product or service.

After all, each author is looking for a style guide to make a clear copy of it, and countless helpful rule books and checklist publications give the authors advice on proper use and a uniform language.

Each writer can remember rules, but it takes a little imagination to get the attention of people.

Don't be concerned with the rules, or your copy may be bad.

COPYWRITING MISTAKES TO AVOID

If you talk to your prospect on your phone or in person, they are likely honest, sincere, and helpful. However, it may not work the same thing if you interact with the same audience by copying or using your website. You can be viewed as a marketing jerk or a poor pitch in your file. Unfortunately, I found some specimens without anyone feeling with a bit of laziness or chill. Eradicating the marketing discussion and producing a successful copy is not easy, but it can be done.

Copywriting is usually an uncommon combination of words that require users to take effective action. Buy or ask for a demo, sign up for a newsletter, and so on.

To make a switch, the prospects need to conclude by accepting that what they get will not be part of mediocrity.

Now say something to me. Did I get your attention? Yes, it's awesome! Now I'll show you how someone else can be grabbed. Comprehend, or pay attention to every aspect your reader can't have it all. Our brain is like this -- the brain must concentrate on all details to comprehend things properly; otherwise, it cannot absorb it all. Then why are you stuck? It is time for your organisation finds compelling and representative examples. We learn some basic yet dangerous pitfalls before we meet when writing text to enhance the quality of your game and educate readers of you.

MISTAKE #1 WRITING FOR YOURSELF

Sometimes you are so obsessed that you don't even realize that something that appeals to your target audience is communicated to you. No, do it never! Ensure that your copy talks about the material to the user so it can be cited easily. This strengthens the loyalty of brands. Such a word can be regarded as a silly but costly mistake in writing to the wrong person, however. Suppose you're selling a family car, for instance. Do not use all fathers to establish gender roles as mothers have the last word.

What can you do? Make a detailed investigation, make sure you touch, and then write.

MISTAKE #2 LONG SALES COPY

A thing of the past is long selling copies! The days when more than 1000 words are read have passed. They skimp today because there is too much content every day to keep everything up. It does not say, though, that you can't use 3,000 random words to await their end-users. It takes all to be good; perhaps great.

Be careful but try a long copy of each word. Do you think your conversion levels can be increased? Otherwise, use sweet and short things. An idea or concept is considered unique only when it exceeds its predecessor, and better and more concise fulfils its function. Continue to track your current website review, especially those recently released. High rebound and low conversions point directly to an optimized copy.

MISTAKE #3 IGNORING SEO

In 2019, more and more copies are available online, as websites are necessary. You should, therefore, be aware that even basic optimization of search engines (SEO) in word creation. Use the term of the search and find out how people look for your product. If you leave these little points, your sales and your web visitors can significantly decrease.

MISTAKE #4 SAYING IT ALL

The content of the long form would contribute to higher rates of conversion. It does not assume, however, that a method will be infinite. To make an excessive copy has become a bit dated with a list of benefits. It certainly has a lot to say, but it might get boring and miss the blow. It sounds like everyone else's, too.

Say more with less. What can be done? Be correct within the content because the attention of the user is not long. For a few sentences as possible, your copy should include the context, one of which I've ever met with the best examples. The headline uses a fast, snappy headline that condenses multiple phrases in three words.

MISTAKE #5 ASSUMPTIONS IS THE MOTHER OF ALL GOOF-UPS

Have you ever considered serving your customers with a dish that includes everything in your company's technical language and style? I think most businesses presume that the technical language of their end readers is very strong. Even if you think that your technical expertise is well presented as a marketer, it doesn't mean that your copy bullies your end-users. You 're not getting anywhere when you use too much jargon or write copy without knowing what your end users want. That doesn't mean, however, that you should not use strong words. Use words that build anxiety, aggression, anticipation, and practice. And how this feeling can also be translated when I say these words of power.

MISTAKE #6 USING STRUCTURE THAT STRANGLES

It is quite easy to write and design several templates, but do you think that these are capable of converting landing pages? If column layouts are like books, I mean multiple layouts such as newspapers that flip and choose what they read and want to ignore.

Within a one-column model, one concept flows to the next. This ensures that your audience can read any word from left to right. You can always use the subtitles, graphics, and text boxes to get readers through the page if you use this process. Even do not use side-by-side text columns but connect it to images. The reasoning here is very straightforward: each line features a text column that requires visitors to read it all.

MISTAKE #7, BELIEVING EVERY BEST PRACTICE.

Not hundreds, but thousands of practices are useful for you. It pays to be careful with the tips given in the writing area. For instance, people often say that readers "never read underneath the fold" or that certain words should be kept making X sales.

When it comes to writing text, there is no solution for anyone. It depends on a given situation, in reality. Use best practices, instead, as a guide or a starting point, not as a start or end, because often a hunch will be better.

MISTAKE #8 BEING TOO FORMAL, STIFF OR BORING

No one who has expertise in English needs to work with you to send you a copy of your sales. Do you think it is possible to sell your product or service if you make an accurate, literary copy with great words and obey the rules strictly? Not definitely! As I said, you have to make your copy so formal that you feel like talking to your best friend. You must be short, simple, and powerful. It's like this if any grammatical laws are mutilated.

It is easy to consume one thought when you write a sales copy: sell it.

However, when writing texts, this approach could be your destiny. Your customer wants a transformation while you want to make a sale.

You may be failing your message if you don't share the transformation vision when you write -- using the "Company" button.

Sales and beyond, you should focus on how to guide your customers securely. Why sales should be focused on is like a hit on the road. I very early accelerated when my trainer commented casually, "Look at the stone on the road."

How exactly was I in my lane to match my tires, and I don't know how it got here.

There was a great deal of variety, but just one issue. He could not get her eyes off him. He could not take his off her. It's been everything I could think of. You know you concentrate on everything when you drive. Several seconds later, my teacher became grey (it was his car), a disgusting hit.

Luckily, no serious damage has occurred. I don't believe I know about cars, but I'm confident they were okay. Then, my instructor wanted to know how I achieved this amazing performance. That is why?

Where we wanted to go, we had two vastly different ideas. He thought of a clear path behind the brick, and all I could see was on the street this next block.

YOUR CUSTOMER DOESN'T THINK ABOUT "SALES."

The writing says, "Be on the two sides of the counter." There is a theory.

This means that you also have to understand the perspective of your customer from their perspective, even if you want to sell from your hand. You will know what the

customer feels before the sale. To do so effectively, for example, my dad could meet an employee who enthusiastically reviewed the clocks and whistles of the device and data plans. If he needed to go to a store to buy a new cell phone, while it may all be thrilling for an expert on telephony, my dad did not think so. My dad believes,
"I have to buy cheaply, quickly, and comfortably, certainly, and then find a tranquil beer bar, pool table, and domino game."

This is also true of your copy of sales. You have trouble writing a connecting copy if you don't know what is important for your client.

THE COPYWRITING FORMULA

Let's get an alert to continue. Let's start. Fear is suited for abuse and manipulation as with any psychologically informed method of persuasion. I assume one thing -- you're going to use this form of writing for good... not for evil.

So the problem solved by your company is a real problem, and its solution is just as real. In other words, it's not only about successfully using terror. There is an acceptable application thereof.

Every content that you create must do two things:

(1) save the audience from its flesh, and
(2) take it to its sky.

Fear is a significant incentive. The most original, Emotional Intelligence author Daniel Goleman says, "Fear has a special meaning in evolution: maybe it is more critical than any emotion."

What does fear have to do with copywriting?

The dominant role of fear is called "lost aversion" by psychologists in day-to-day decisions. The underlying concept is simple -- people want loss instead of profit to be prevented. It is more the risk of injury than the prospect of victory that motivates us. And, of course, aversion and avoidance are synonymous with fear where fear triumphs over hope, but more explicitly, day after day and Sunday twice a week. The copywriting, contents and marketing effects of this knowledge are tremendous, and for years, intelligent marketers have used fear.

You'll know how incredibly effective this first formula is if you understand that people behave to avoid pain rather than winning.

In all imaginable business areas, from security systems to skincare products, I used this basic formula to structure super-efficient sales presentations of live vendors. I used it not only for sales letters but also for sellers in over 136 different industries. Perhaps the trusted sales formula that has ever been invented. The structure is as follows:

PROBLEM: Define the problem as easily as possible, often in one sentence. You just have to nod and glide straight to the next lines for your reader. Clarify the issue clearly and directly: just say sufficient to agree here.

AGITATION: While they believe the problem is a problem, but it is not a true nightmare. Here it must come to life. Fantastic. It is time to produce emotions until the question is transparent and real. There was a mistake. Using your anger, your resentment, your guilt, your shame, your fear, your genuine negative emotions, you need readers to wring hands mentally, walk around the room, and say, "They have to stop! I must do something about it! I must do something about it! What can I do about it? If there's just an answer!"

SOLUTION: After Hell, comes Heaven. The third step is to show the solution, the response, and the advantages of your product or service.

The problem is that most marketing measures are step two turmoil.

We recognize the problem and go straight to the solution without stopping to drive home. What's going on? Concentrate on simplicity and coherence in step one. Show your audience that you understand their fear and show that, if necessary, the problem is a matter of fact. Concentrate on emotions and volatility in step two. It needs to become real now that the problem has been identified. It means to be firmly pressed.

POWER OF STORYTELLING
IN MARKETING

The power of storytelling is not a technique, a process, or a method. Storytelling is considered to be art -- storytelling, "art." Like art, creativity, vision, competence, and practice are required. A course in all of history can't be understood simultaneously. This is a method that fixes the mistake.

It does not sound like a lot of work. And with good reason, because telling stories has been included in the most successful marketing campaigns. Distinguish between pure, lively brands and loyal buyers. We're drawn to the lessons, the exciting trips, the vision that we get, and the ability to unleash our imagining, from childhood to adulthood.

The stories celebrate our culture, and the stories bear witness to our lives. The stories make transmitting messages easier. Remember that excellent teacher, who told stories about what he teaches and how those stories made it easier than this boring teacher, who just "taught," and you probably forgot his name. Who was that teacher? After all, we are social animals with the language to communicate, to express emotions, to understand, and even to become simple, the world around us and ourselves. Data list to control data and information to track history and interpretation information and information on specified subjects.

When you tell your brand's story, you should explain who your voice is, what it means, and why it matters to the audience's lives who have their history. Complete the steps and show readers how to recognize the prize. Sales should be imaginative but mostly subtle and indirect.

It is the centre of inbound marketing as well. The narrative is an essential basis for proverbial marketing. This is why I compiled this guide to help you to discover and learn storytelling and to teach your audiences beautiful, unchangeable stories.

History of history, life's history, and the fact that it is manual, the basic principles of ongoing marketing are outlined. You will take them to a place that they want to follow for a long time by giving your goods and services an identity by catching and sharing the stories that they are. If consumers are to connect to their brand personality, the stories of the company must be genuine, creative, and inspiring.

Emotional branding is a sophisticated marketing tactic that stimulates revenue and improves the loyalty of consumers. How an individual feels about your brand usually determines if they buy your product. A brand is a question of perspective. You create an experience that engages your customers when you tell a story that poses human challenges.

Remembrance is not a narrative. Why it has developed products and services and why it does what it does is full of history, is why your company exists.

You want to meet needs, respond to questions, emotionally engage, communicate, find your voice, and listen to voices at the interface of the company, and the public. The way you developed solutions and offered value is about storytelling. A meeting of conversions and solutions for internal narratives that tell stories with which people can identify.

Storytelling can focus on a particular project and also write and produce content that combines personal and current stories with the storytelling of the brand. Some people say that everything good tells a story. This is a myth. Content must be informative sometimes. You, your brand, and your solutions/products are not even good storytelling. It is about the emotions, experiences, and needs of your brand and the written and unwritten images associated with those emotions and needs.

Storytelling is not only about coherence and adaptation to changing human needs, although sometimes it seems that certain actions and projects have a unique dimension, but everything from events and content to campaigns always fits into this broader narrative. Finally, note that, by nature, the narrative is autonomous and personalized.

A captivating brand story, like a fairy tale, must include three acts that describe the situation, document the conflict, and provide a solution. Business accounts are, however, unique as they need a fourth element -- an often indirect call to action.

The ultimate objective of Marketing is to motivate change, encourage a product to be purchased, or attract people for your company, regardless of the time frame. At the end of the day, the desired outcome determines the direction. The stories must be human and personal.

Consider how your brand came into being, what motivated you to start the business, and your mission? Think of the needs of the "audience," in particular.

The story must be impressive and often purposeful. While it is important to tell your own story, customer stories affect brands most long term. The consumer wants to be the main character and to help the organization build successful solutions as a supporting character with tools.

In a campaign to buy new playground equipment, for example, for a community centre, the message needs to focus on why and who will benefit from that equipment. Concentrate on one or two recipients and show their lives what the donation means. Lobbying should always come from someone else, not from a company spokesperson, in the form of a quote.

Witness accounts can be your best tool if you are instructed correctly to build customer loyalty. A story consisting of a couple of sentences is memorable, but one that addresses a customer's personal life and demonstrates how long an employee takes to solve the problem and shows how good the results are long after changing a customer, you are going to receive promotional information.

Any standard, such as forums, videos, mass media, social media, and multimedia, can be used to tell stories. The different reactions triggered by the audience must be adapted to meet your needs. Knowing which story to say in which medium is the key to success. Short, fast messages are best for TV, the Internet and personal connections are established by conversation, conference, and webinars.

You have to listen to your audience to be a good storyteller so you can appreciate their desires and fears, values, and attitudes. When your tale unfolds, you will always listen to the reactions of your audience. Allow your brand to decide how this develops. As your goals change, new initiatives must be planned which promote the history and encourage new calls to action. Emotions, authenticity, personal links, and readiness to act; that's what storytelling means, and the old infographic of storytelling is still relevant in this sense.

There have been no improvements to the laws of the narration, the framework, and the integrated approach. Yet listening always begins, and it's not about talking.

WHY STORYTELLING IS SUCH A POWERFUL MARKETING COMMUNICATIONS STRATEGY

It's not new storytelling. As social media and content marketing channels are continuing to grow, in terms of numbers and value, storytelling has never been a big part of strategic marketing strategies. We have to sell ideas, knowledge, and reputation as communication partners. The stories help you conquer the mentalities and dynamics of marketing a good or service; and if the audience links to your marketing tales, it results in approval, both figuratively (brand trust) and literally (product sales).

HOOK YOUR AUDIENCE EARLY

Start your story by catching their attention using a question or presenting a problem to solve.

The best stories address the public's problems, lift their curiosity, and keep them sufficiently motivated to read more. Like a fairy tale, three acts in a captivating brand story determine the situation, record the conflict, and offer a solution.

MAKE YOUR CUSTOMER THE PROTAGONIST, NOT YOUR PRODUCT

The main character of your story is your client. The support personnel are your business. A mediocre narrator differs from a good one in personal relevance. Give the public apart, and you can see it as an extension of your brand narrative.

While this is not a product or service in your story, it might be part of it. Think of stories from large brands like Target or IKEA, who know people want a style for their home on a tight budget.

CONNECT WITH THE EMOTIONAL IMPACT

Our customers are people, not rational beings, naturally. We often decide and then create reasonable arguments. We make decisions based on feelings, in other words. The brand's narrative has a psychological dimension, and emotions are an important element. It is difficult to get others to take care of things without an emotional bond.

Do you remember, "This is your drug brain" nonprofit campaign? Now, it's resurrected for a new generation, but the basic and alarming message of the original cannot be overlooked. A spectacular example that our brains understand the structure of history implicitly. Complete the gaps that have not been told. In comparison to our thought processes that can only be slowly created, our emotional mind is incredibly resourceful.

THERE IS AN ART TO CONTENT CREATION

Thanks to technology, our clients, their models, and even human emotions that cause the need for buying have been better understood, but the business is personal at the end of the day, and we buy brands we like and have confidence and trust. Storytelling continues to demonstrate its ability to help businesses and their communicators create and sustain such relationships with consumers, thus increasing our business and brand.

IMPORTANCE OF STORYTELLING IN MARKETING

We have always told stories, and they are a significant part of our everyday contact, but stories are meaningless. The narration is a great business skill. It can improve an organization in a variety of ways if successfully implemented, including Customer loyalty enhancement and the development of a successful marketing campaign, benefits increase, etc.

The storytelling is everywhere; in podcasts, radio, books, articles, TV, and the time that his friend's sister kissed the famous soccer player In his best moment. All the storytelling details were there. A good story can have a huge effect on our minds and allow us to get there and make us forget about the world around us.

A well-told good story affects our brains physically -- knowing a set of facts as part of an entertaining tale takes more of the brains and requires more neurons than the facts mentioned. Losing yourselves in history is indeed a mechanism of survival firmly anchored in us, to better store data.

Most of our job as marketers is to see, note, and recall our goods. So, what could be better than sharing stories to deliver a message that will draw so attract the attention of our chosen audience as long as possible? The key factors of the importance of storytelling in marketing are listed below.

POWER

Storytelling will communicate with your audience by using your customer as the narrator and your product as a solution to a problem. This enables the value of your product to be transmitted clearly. It is an enormously powerful tool since the beginning of time and in all life phases, people have been connected by stories.

MEMORY

The message is easier to remember. Instead of being bombarded with facts, people recall stories that relate to a real experience. It's that easy when something brings us to feel an emotion we remember best.

It is a unique approach. You can make the consumer, not your product, a protagonist by engaging him at a deeper neurological level through the magic of storytelling. You will then stand out without having a greater or louder sound from the crowded advertising environment but by stimulating the brain more productively and permanently.

We recall stories that are more engaging than other types of information, such as data and facts. Knowledge and information have been primarily transmitted in oral stories before papers and computers, and more than half of human conversation is carried out through narration. This is the natural part that we think and communicate.

Telling a story gives the viewer a break when you make a lecture or lecture. Since the stories are timeless, at least the audience can remember the story, even if you forget it.

BUSINESS DEVELOPMENT

There's a story behind it if you have an idea about your business, either by creating a new product or by through your company. Tell this story and provide your customers and stakeholders with a context to understand why your service or product should be bought or invested in by them. Let them know the importance of your story behind the product.

He developed his idea to solve a problem. Say how this issue impacts you and how your product/service has been accomplished. Make the story in real-life situations accessible to the public, as this will help you see why your products add value to your lives.

This narrative allows the public to connect with you, to trust you, the individual, and the brand. In particular, the story is very understandable, and it also has the benefit of being easier to understand and more memorable because it is relevant personally. The audience can consider themselves as the character in the story.

COMPETITIVE ADVANTAGE

So much information is available to consumers that a company is lost in the noise. A company can sell more than its rivals, but the decisions are more emotional than rational. So you can tell a story apart from the competition when you tell a story.

Researchers showed the value of storytelling with warm and dedicated short stories by auctioning out insignificant items on eBay. The products, purchased for approximately $1.25, were sold for almost $8,000 cumulatively. This shows how an intelligent approach to storytelling can increase the perceived value and generate ROI.

MAINTAINS ATTENTION AND INCREASES UNDERSTANDING

The tales are quite amazing. No matter if you use a story in a market, ad, etc., you will lose your audience's attention less likely. Therefore, speeches often begin with storytelling.

Stories are also highly structured forms of communication that encourage audience understanding.

MARKETING AND ADVERTISING

Storytelling can be a strong marketing strategy. People want to connect to brands and companies, and the best ads can do so through emotions, like John Lewis in the UK or the Budweiser ad. This can be a powerful marketing strategy. More than cheap strategies, like sex attraction or must-reads.

A successful advertisement for brands always needs to be available. Tell people what the commercial battle was like and how it succeeded (the monolithic story). It causes the public to look after you and also your product or service. Make sure that all media maintain this story consistently in public announcements, social healthcare, your web, your employees, etc. You want the audience and the brand's past to appreciate your dream.

INCREASES EMPLOYEE EFFICIENCY AND ENGAGEMENT

Employees are the core of the business; they are the greatest asset for the organization, and an organization only succeeds if its employees do so. Work, however, shows that there is widespread involvement. Gallup's study, for example, shows that 70 percent of American employees are not working or actively laid off from jobs.

Telling stories can keep the right culture at work. This goes beyond the sharing of a successful vision, but more like sharing history, struggles, values, goals, etc. Tell your workers what it means to them and explain to them what it means. This gives them something to believe in, and consequently, they will believe in the company and will increase their motivation to work.

In essence, it gives the workers a greater sense of mission by integrating them into the broader history of the company. To further develop that by allowing your employees to share their own stories.

DECISION-MAKING

People's quest for decision tales. If you think, for instance, about buying a product, consider reviews which are essentially stories, not just facts, and details. This also goes for business. When people think, "Why should I get involved?" they try to think about why they are looking for stories.

To answer the simple question, "Why should people care?" Every company has to use storytelling to call on clients, potential employees, or stakeholders.

HUMANISING A BRAND AND INCREASING PROFIT

The most successful companies, including *Google* and Apple, are not just companies; they're innovative brands that want to transform the world. They also have profound and insightful stories behind them. You would be more likely to be successful if you have a dream that the public will trust and buy.

People want to purchase from companies they think, D. H. Companies that are sensitive. The Global Empathy Index (2015) highlighted this fact, where companies rank among the world's most profitable and rapidly growing firms. The top ten enterprises also made 50 percent more sales and doubled the value of the last ten. Use storytelling to show your company empathy because your company is more likely to succeed.

Through social media, people can now directly contact brands, ask questions, and share their thoughts and feelings as if the brand is an individual. Tell a good story to show your business's personality and humanity-do not just become a facial business where customers do not feel unconnected, uninspired, interact with, or shop.

TRANSFER VALUES AND BELIEFS ON TO YOUR AUDIENCE

You can create beliefs by showing people how you believed anything when people care about their stories. The transmission of values and faiths is done by the nature of his story, which has a revelation because it is also experienced by his audience. Take what you know, believe it, and put to your audience's attention to your product/service.

EMOTIONALLY CONNECT PEOPLE AND CREATE LOYALTY

The best stories evoke emotional reactions. These stories are addressed and connected. They believe in and what the business is all about. If you listen to an audiobook novel, you feel what the narrator feels. One perfect way to communicate with the audience with a story is to tell the tale of a mistake made by or the company, a loss, or even the life, or the business. In the past, it wasn't healthy.

We all have errors and weaknesses. People should notice it. The more people talk to you or understand what helped to create the brand, the more likely you and your organization will like them. The more they like them. Note that people typically make emotional decisions rather than logical ones. It is thus a strong instrument for evoking emotions by telling stories. Put your dream into a compelling tale and express it with a truthful marketing strategy.

STORIES CREATE PURPOSE AND DRIVE ACTION

The stories give meaning and reason for the audience to act. The Wharton School of Business (2007), for example, found that those who were told how the money would change other people's lives gained more than twice the group who were told what money was like. Participants were told to raise donations that they wished would better their own lives at a call centre. The sense of purpose meant he earned more from the first group. So just tell stories if you want to trigger actions.

CONCLUSION

Today, a popular brand that has no story behind it is difficult to find. Stories create meaning, context, and meaning. History makes sense. Many people are more sensitive than facts or dates to stories because stories allow us to recognize, to sympathize, and to recall. That is why the value of telling stories is recognized by more and more businesses.

PRINCIPLES OF STORYTELLING

To tell stories effectively, we need to understand a bit why the stories connect and how to communicate through listening and storytelling.

Tales influence the human psyche almost magically. Stories can entertain, touch our hearts, and enlighten the world we live.

A sophisticated brand tale is perfect for chatting, getting in touch with an audience, and creating loyalty. Apply these principles as you create a story that helps people remember your brand and perhaps even fall in love.

HUMANS ARE HARDWIRED FOR STORY

To teach one another life, we use stories, and a community was formed where we share these stories. Storytelling is a way of recording and transmitting culture, as cultures rely on communication to allow transmission from generation to generation. In thousands of years, this primitive way of telling stories has become a more internally meaningful way of telling stories.

Storytelling is often claimed to be the most effective and powerful form of human communication because it is embedded directly in our brain equipment. The story is how the brain helps us understand our lives and build consistency from chance and chaos. Most of our awareness, experience, and thought is structured as a novel. It's our way of intertwining, by means of memory, with our past to understand what happened to us and plan a future in which we can imagine certain results.

Scientists have made exciting discoveries of our brain's ability to tell and understand history to support theories that storytelling is a neurobiological feature. Experiments with people on PET scanners were conducted to capture real-time brain activity images. Some areas of the brain are lit up by listening to different kinds of information. If somebody listens to a list of shopping, some brain area lights up. Another part of the brain lights up when the person listens to a song, but when someone hears a story or tells a story, a number of certain brain areas are lit.

Patients with brain damage to certain areas are also clear evidence that they are unable to say or respond to stories.

This means that the brain is designed to tell and listen to stories in certain places.

What is it really about brain wiring? It means a network of brain cells involved in the telling of tales. They are wired even more effectively when they are shot. The narration is one way of enhancing these brain links. It's a talent that can be built, a muscle that can be consolidated. In work we have carried out over the last two, and a half decade, we have seen ample evidence of this. The more stories you tell, the better you understand them.

EVERYONE HAS A STORY

I've never found anyone who has zero history in all the years I did this work. I will tell you, without hesitation, that something has taken place in your life that is a fantastic story if you do not feel your story is significant or urgent enough, or if you believe those in your company are the storytellers. Each participant comes across a story that truly describes a life event after completing our workshops, regardless of age and storytelling. After these events, we just have to know how to dig.

We recommend that you start training first to find a personal story. A story explaining how you reached your site can be particularly successful. This is what we call your "Tale of birth." You will tell the story after you have witnessed the cycle of telling a story near you. This means you can use for business purposes all the emotional powers and effects of personal history.

EVERYONE CAN LEARN TO TELL HIS OR HER STORY BETTER

We believe that only time and practice can improve your storytelling skills, but if you follow what happened to your story, the procedure can make a quantum leap forward for your narrative. This is a completely straightforward system. It says not to make things material about what has happened, the interpretations, the opinions, the judgments, the abstraction, and the concept of what has happened. It is this proven and compelling content that absorbs your senses. When you say, "What happened?" You must tell your story to listeners from start to finish. Follow these directions.

The method as a basis, it is undoubtedly an art form with many parts to tell a story well. Scenes and people must be conjured up, the voices modulated, and the audience moved around the room.

EVERYONE'S STORY WILL EVOLVE

You may already know how to tell a story, and you might believe that the story you said was the last. You once or twice told the manager, and all of them applauded. And why not say more to the winner?

We never advise against using a story with a well-known history, but we keep the door open, so your story is likely to evolve. It evolves in various listening environments so that you can customize your message as you speak, see how the audience reacts, and develop your story. A good story inevitably unfolds and represents the mutual relationship between listening and speaking. The contact spark is a good story.

STORYTELLING IS EVERY PERSON'S ACCESS TO CREATIVITY

Creativity is long regarded as the province of artists or as a region of talents and special talents. Still, we know now that creativity is also an integral element of humanity. The most important definition is creativity, the "recovery of existing elements in a new, surprising manner."

Storytelling is the most democratic form of creativity since it is available to everyone. Your birthright story is yours and yours alone. By paying attention to specific details, you will always create something new and if you learn to tell your story artistically, many people, will read it. For example, many people have fallen in love, but none of them experienced love. You have a great chance to make creative choices when telling your story. You can look at or zoom in and see some details. When creating your story, you can make the most of every sense.

The good thing about storytelling is that you have a business story or a personal story with the creativity and freedom of expression.

THERE IS A RECIPROCAL RELATIONSHIP BETWEEN LISTENING AND TELLING

Unless we feel that anyone is listening to and observing us, we can't tell a story. For the same reason, unless the narrator knows his audience rather than being trapped in the bubble of his speech, we cannot hear a story. There is a reciprocal relationship between listening and counting in this most fundamental context. The essence of the narrative approach is this idea. It sounds straightforward, and it is. You will learn more and more about how this affects your communication by paying attention. Our method offers a means to sensitize the audience and narrator about this dynamic relationship and use it for effective stories.

We frequently think that narration is mainly about the abilities in presentation, but only part of this ability. We believe that listening is of equal, if not of greater importance. It is simply not possible to tell stories without them. Therefore, in our work with businesses, we also look at the communication climate.

LEAD GENERATION

Sensitivity online today can be a real challenge, let alone an online draw for more customers. On average, visitors linger just 15 seconds on websites, and most will never return. If you have invested considerable resources on traffic capture, most can be lost if you do not do so properly. That's why top marketers often preach about the value of list formation. To do this, you will create an email list of guides and customers to create and promote them on an ongoing basis, but will you create your email list effectively? Or, are you simply giving your audience a chance to sign up for your newsletter?

A lead Magnet gives potential customers in exchange for an e-mail address and possibly other kinds of information, like name and telephone number. You have to build an email list if you are successful in gaining online customers and you need a lead magnet to create an email list effectively. You make a free offer in return for an e-mail address and maybe further information with a lead-magnet.

It's labelled an "irresistibly bribe" by a known digital marketer. Board leading magnets were also an important weapon in the seller's arsenal. In the digital age, they are particularly beautiful, as we are readers and make requests instantly.

The purpose of a lead magnet is to encourage people to add their content to your email list. Use parenting tactics, especially e-mail, to make the customers in the future. Lead magnets are an integral part of the content marketing strategy, cultivating a loyal audience, and developing the company efficiently.

WHAT MAKES A GOOD LEAD MAGNET?

High Perceived Value: If you do not consider a desirable subscription to a big magnet, most of your target audiences are not drawn to a free newsletter campaign. Your main magnet has to be seen as very precious or better yet must have high true value depending on the type of market in which you work.

Instant Gratification: Your audience is always in search of a solution. In no time, create an email list, if your primary magnet can close this distance.

Demonstrates Your Unique Selling Proposition: If your audience absorbs the magnet, they should also be encouraged more to buy from you instead of from their rivals.

Why Lead Magnets Work?

One of your goals is to raise awareness, build confidence, and reputation as a digital marketing specialist. However, it can be difficult to calculate the effectiveness of these initiatives.

Therefore, lead magnets should be provided. We are the ideal bridge for potential buyers who never learned about your company in return for useful items to send them their e-mail addresses.

Lead magnets can also support potential buyers by asking them to commit themselves, in particular, if they can fill in a form that needs more than just an e-mail address.

Examples of Lead Magnets

1. Samples
2. Training Videos
3. Templates
4. Courses
5. Quizzes
6. Case Studies
7. Coupons/Discount Codes
8. Software
9. Checklist
10. Webinar

The last magnet can be a webinar. Every day, I receive several webinar invitations. Do you? They are sometimes filled with bravery. Not usually. In 99 percent of cases, however, they are safe. The success secrets. Build an invaluable and free webinar. Big magnetic titles webinars accomplish their first goal to produce e-mail leads.

Superb webinars and other excellent sites include much more. Would you:

- Make customers participants
- Improves loyalty and commitment
- Encourage existing and new customers to support them.

Some Webinar Tips:

- Submit your experience, your industry experts in different areas, or invite you to the lecture. Make a special offer free of charge or paid to reward participants.
- When you establish ties with other significant companies, provide your audience with webinars. The host usually answers with the e-mail addresses of the registrant.

WHAT IS THE LEAD?

A potential customer is anyone who shows an interest in a company's product or service in any way, in any way, or in any way.

Potential customers often hear from a company or organization after opening communications by sending personal information for an offer, trial, or subscription instead of receiving a random call from someone who purchased their contact information.

Let's say you're taking an online survey to learn more about caring for your car. About a day later, you receive an email from the auto company that created the survey on how it can help you take care of your car. This process would be much less intrusive than if you had been called out of the blue without knowing if you even took care of car maintenance, right? This is how to be a leader.

From a business perspective, the information the car company gathers about you from your survey responses helps to personalize this opening communication to solve your existing problems, and you don't waste time calling potential customers who are not interested In auto services.

Leads are part of the broader life cycle that consumers follow as they transition from visitor to customer. Not all potential customers are the same and are not equally qualified. There are different types of leads, depending on how qualified they are and what phase of their life cycle they are at the time.

Such lead generators are just a few examples of lead-generation techniques you can use to draw and deliver leads. I can't just say, "I'm producing content for lead generation," if someone outside of the marketing world asks me what I'm doing. I could get very curious looks. I would like to sell you more goods to engage you naturally in my business so that they can contact the brand because they want 'us' to hear it!' I say, "I'm looking for innovative ways of attracting customers to my company. This is usually best received, and that is exactly what the lead is about. This allows you to warm up and make a purchase for your company.

WHY DO YOU NEED LEAD GENERATION?

If a stranger establishes a relationship with you with organic interest in your business, the transition is much more natural from an alien to a customer. The second phase of the inbound marketing methodology involves the production of leaders. This happens once you have drawn an audience and are ready for the sales team (i.e., qualified sales leaders) to turn those visitors into guides.

As you can see in the figure below, lead generation is a key step in becoming an exciting customer.

LEAD GENERATION PROCESS

Now that we know how lead generation suits the inbound marketing approach, we are following the steps in lead generation.

- Next, a visitor can discover your business through a marketing platform, for example, your website, forum, or webpage.
- The visitor clicks on an image, button, or message that invites visitors to the website to take action.
- This CTA leads the visitor to a landing page, a website that offers lead information in exchange for a bid.

Note: The material or something that is "offered" on the landing page, for example, is an offer, a course, or a free sample download. The deal must have sufficient perceived value to allow visitors to provide their personal information in exchange for access.

- You will complete a form in exchange for the offer as soon as you are on the landing page. (Forms are usually hosted at landing pages, but they can theoretically be integrated into the site anywhere.) Voila! You've got a new profit. This is so long as you follow best practices for forms of lead selection.

See how anything fits?

To sum up, you click on a CTA to take you to a landing page where you fill out an offer form. They will be the chief from this moment on with their interaction.

By the way, look at our tool to create free leads. You can use it directly on your website for creating lead capture forms. The configuration is also straightforward.

LEAD GENERATION MARKETING

You can use your various advertising platforms, once you've put this together, to carry traffic to your landing page and generate leads.

Your landing page, what channels should you use? Let's discuss the front-end of lead generation: the marketing of lead genes.

This chart shows the flow of commercial marketing channels to a generated lead, as you visually learn. More leads are available to make visitors lead. Let's take a closer look and discuss some more.

CONTENT

Content is an ideal way of reaching consumers. It generates content to provide visitors with useful and free information. Anywhere in your content, you can insert CTA -- online, at the end of the post, in the hero, or even in the page area. The more interesting a visitor is, the more likely they are to click on your application to continue and move to your destination page.

E-MAIL

E-mail is a great place to talk to people who know your brand, product, or department. Such as they are already on your mind, it is much easier to ask them to do something. Typically, e-mails are a little frustrating. So use CTA to attract your subscribers' attention with an attractive copy and a spectacular design.

ADS AND RETARGETING

An ad is designed solely to make users act. If not, why donate the money? Make sure that your landing page and the promised values in the ad suit your users want to convert, and you have specific behaviour.

BLOG

The best way to promote an offer with your blog posts is to adapt the entire work to the final goal. So, you can write an article on how to choose your marketing metricians if your offer is an instructional video to set up *Google* Search Console. This is extremely important and easy to click on your CTA.

SOCIAL MEDIA

You can easily guide your followers in action by using social media platforms, from the swipe up option on Instagram stories to biographical Facebook links and small Twitter URLs. Through your social contributions, you can also advertise your bid and include an action call in your lyrics. Further information can be found in this article on social media campaigns.

PRODUCT TRIALS

Through providing trial versions of your product or service, you will remove several obstacles to sales. Once your product is used by a prospective client, you can be tempted to purchase it with additional offers or resources. It is also recommended to include your brand in its free versions so that other potential customers can be drawn.

REFERRAL MARKETING

Mouth marketing reference or term is helpful to produce lead. This means you have more customers in front of your brand, and your chances of producing more leads increase.

Whichever channel you used to generate leads, your users would like to take you to your landing page. The rest takes care of itself, as long as you have created a landing page that converts.

WHY NOT JUST BUY LEADS?

Marketers want to fill up their funnel similarly, and they want to complete it quickly.

In comparison to organic production, buying leads is much simpler and takes a lot less time and effort, although they are more costly, but perhaps you are still paying for advertising. Why not buy leads, then?

You don't know all of the leads you purchased first. They usually "check-in" to another location than when they subscribed and didn't choose to receive something.
The messages you send are, therefore, spam messages and e-mails. Remember that upsetting call I received when I was trying to eat spaghetti? This is the way people feel when they get emails from people that they don't want to hear. If your potential customer has never visited your website and is interested in your products or services, simply stop, both and just.

If you've never wanted to receive your messages directly, it's safe to mark your messages as spam, which is very risky. Not only does this train filter emails from you, but it also indicates which emails are to be filtered.

As soon as many people recognize your messages as spam, go to a blacklist and exchange them with other email providers. It is very hard to get rid of it once you're blacklisted. Also, it is possible to affect your e-mail and IP reputation. Increased organic production is often better than buying them.

HOW TO QUALIFY A LEAD

As we mentioned in the first segment, a potential consumer has shown an interest in the product or service of your business. Now let's think about how this passion can be conveyed.

The key benefit of collecting knowledge is revenue. This collection will result from a job seeker searching for a work, who trades contact information for a voucher, or who completes the form for downloading the course material. This information can be the product of an application process.

LEAD SCORING

Lead scoring is a quantitative approach to qualification. This procedure gives the potential customer a numerical value (or sample) to determine the scale of "ready to sell" for the "interested." The criteria for these promotions are entirely yours, but in your marketing and sales department, they must be consistent so that everyone works on the same scale.

A customer's potential score can be based on the action, the information they provide, brand commitment, or other criteria that their sales team sets. For example, if you have daily social media interactions with you or if your demographic data suits your target group, you might score someone else.

You may use one of its coupons in following the above examples to give a leader a higher score, which means that an individual is interested in your product.

The higher the lead ranking, the closer the customer is to sell a Successful Lead (SQL). Up to the formula that works, you might need to change your score and criteria. Once you do this, your lead generation will be changed into a customer generation.

LEAD GENERATION STRATEGIES

Online lead generation consists of many techniques, promotions, and approaches, depending on the site. When you have a visitor to your website, we discuss best practices to capture a lead. But how are you able to take them?
See leaders for some common platforms in generation strategies.

FACEBOOK LEAD GENERATION

Since its inception, Facebook is a leading generational method. Companies could initially use outbound links in their BIOS posts and information to attract foreigners. The way companies used their platform to track leads was greatly changed as Facebook ads started in 2007, and their algorithm began to favour accounts that use paid advertising. Facebook has produced lead ads for this purpose. Facebook has a feature that allows you to position the Facebook folders to your site directly on the top of your Facebook page, by placing a simple call to action button.

TWITTER LEAD GENERATION

Twitter has Twitter Lead Generation Cards to create tweets without having to leave the web. A user's name, email address and Twitter username are dragged to the wallet. Only press "Send" to become a future customer.

LINKEDIN LEAD GENERATION

Since its foundation, LinkedIn has increased its involvement in the publicity space. When a user is clicked on to simplified information entry, LinkedIn generated lead gene types, which are automatically complemented by user profile data.

PPC LEAD GENERATION

We mean advertisements on the results of the search engine (SERP) pages when we say pay per click (PPC). *Google* receives every day 3.5 billion search queries, making it the best asset for any ad campaign, particularly lead genes. The success of your PPC campaign depends mainly on continuing user experience, budget, keywords, and some additional factors.

TIPS FOR LEAD GENERATION CAMPAIGNS

For any lead generation program, there can be many moving pieces. Through parts of the campaign work and which change is required may be difficult to understand.

What exactly is a lead generation engine? What exactly? Some tips for lead gene campaigns are given here.

USE THE RIGHT LEAD GENERATION TOOLS.

The most successful marketing teams use a structured structure to coordinate and store their results, as you can see from our data. Here are tools for lead generation and applications for lead generation.

How much are you aware of the visits to your website? Do you know the names or addresses of your emails? How do you work and what you do before and after you have completed a conversion form? How are you doing on other sites?

You may find it hard to connect with the people who are on your website if you do not know the answers to these questions. These questions and the appropriate tools for lead development should be accessible to you.

CREATE AMAZING OFFERS FOR ALL DIFFERENT STAGES OF THE BUYING CYCLE.

Not everybody who visits your website is prepared to speak to your sales staff or see your product demo. Anyone who is more familiar with your business and who has a deeper understanding of the company at the end of the trip will be more interested in an invitation, a free trial, or a trial guide at the start of the trip.

Make sure you build proposals for each process and have CTAs on your website for these offerings.

Yeah, it takes time to build precious content which teaches and promotes your funnel leads. However, you can never return to your website if you don't offer visitors who are not willing to buy anything.

KEEP YOUR MESSAGING CONSISTENT AND DELIVER ON YOUR PROMISE.

The highest conversion rate lead campaigns to achieve what they promise and build a smooth transition from the ad and product design to the outcome itself. Make sure that everybody receives a consistent message throughout your lead capture and provides added value.

The aspects of your lead gen campaign should all be reflected in your website, blog, and product. If not, the next step of the life cycle would be difficult for you. Your campaign should not only involve receiving an email address but also winning a new client.

USE SOCIAL MEDIA STRATEGICALLY

In general, marketing experts find social media the best marketing to achieve high-level marketing. Still, as described in previous lead-gene strategies, it can also be a cost-efficient and accessible source of lead. The aim is to use social networks strategically for the development of leads.

First of all, add links on your Facebook, Twitter, LinkedIn, and other social media posts to the landing pages of compelling offers. Please inform visitors to the landing page. You set goals in this way.

You can also perform a lead generation analysis to find out which articles generate most results and then connect them regularly to social media posts.

Competition is also an alternative way to generate social network leads. For your friends, competitions are enjoyable and exciting. You can show your audience a lot, too. It's a win-win scenario.

Your approach for lead generation should be as diverse as the target people. The changes in patterns, attitudes, views, change If the leading attributes of the market shift too. Using split A/B tests to find out which CTAs perform best, which landing pages convert best and which copy is being captured by your audience. Experiment with changes in the design, layout, content, and ad channel until you learn what works.

INFLUENCER MARKETING

What is marketing influence, and, most importantly, should you use it for your brand?

Marketing can push even the hardest entrepreneurs to the wall. Building a brand, speaking your target group's language, selecting the right platforms for your product, and finding out which marketing strategies are most effective for your target market may be a real challenge. Yet you needn't do it on your own. Influence marketing is a perfect way to meet new demands, raise brand awareness, and increase ROI and the bottom line of marketing.

This first chapter provided an overview of influencer marketing from the question of what an influencer is, to choosing the right person, to achieve maximum ROI with influencer marketing and the search for legitimate influencers. In addition to the most significant lesson, we have learned about how powerful a marketing influencer can be on for your product or business.

You are much more likely to do the same when you see celebrities and other famous people who want to wear or wear stuff.

On Instagram, Snapchat, or *YouTube*, the influencers you see on social media have several hundred thousand, or more than one million followers. These people have built up their deserved audience, so they are called influencers. Building followers is really hard to do. *YouTube* and Facebook are paying decent money to those people because they have a substantial organic audience.

INFLUENCER MARKETING

The method of online marketing has become well-established. It has long been a motto, and mainstream media frequently speak it. Nevertheless, there are still people who do not understand all about influencer marketing. Some people first meet with priests and immediately think, "What is marketing influencer?"

The Influencer Marketing Home is now a website with hundreds of items that explain how complex influencer marketing and other forms of online marketing are. The first article we wrote for the site was the original version of this post. We note, however, that people still come here to think about influencer marketing for the first time. This article has been updated to focus on the fundamentals of influencer marketing by 2020.

WHAT ARE INFLUENCERS?

Marketing dynamics were a blend of ancient and modern marketing instruments. He uses the concept of popular ads in a conventional content-oriented campaign. Influencer marketing differentiates primarily from the fact that the strategy resulted in brand and power partnerships.

Marketing influences does not only involve famous people. They are influential individuals who, in an offline environment, would never consider many of them to be famous.

The disparity between famous people and online influencers is one of the most significant errors mainstream media make.

Furthermore, we must recognize that influential people have created an exciting and exciting audience. It's no coincidence that these people do not follow the brand. In reality, your brand does not matter to the public. They think just about influencers' views. Do not try to impose an influencer on business rules and practices. There's the public, and they can go and bring their followers.

WHAT IS INFLUENCER MARKETING?

Promotion influence includes a brand that collaborates in the promotion of one of its goods or services with an online impact. Some partnerships in shaping markets are less measurable. Brands only work to raise brand recognition with influencers.

The *YouTube* popular PewDiePie was an early example of influencer marketing. He collaborated with the makers of a horror film set in Paris' French catacombs and developed a series of videos that presented him with challenges in the catacombs. It was flawless content and almost twice the number of views that Pew Die Pie had for 27 million subscribers. Both of them won.

This is a straightforward case. Even if the start-up is a 10-minute video series, it is easy to imagine a celebrity partnering with a company to show a product.

However, if the marketing power is not commonly used, people wouldn't think about it, you wouldn't read about it on a platform called the Influencer Marketing Hub and the main influencer is in that term.

Influencers can be anywhere, unlike celebrities. You can be anyone. Their big fan base on the web and in social media makes them influential. A well-read cybersecurity blogger who tweets and a respected marketing administrator on LinkedIn may be a famous fashion photographer on Instagram. You only have to find influencers in every industry. Some of them will be followed by hundreds of thousands, if not millions, but more like regular people, others will emerge.

In some cases, you can only have 10,000 followers. Nevertheless, they will have a reputation as experts. They are the contacts who answer questions from people. They are the people who make the most engaging social contributions to your particular subject, depending on their area of expertise. They share the best images, make the videos most entertaining, and discuss online the most informatively.

WHAT WORKS IN INFLUENCER MARKETING

CAREFULLY CONSIDER YOUR APPROACH TO INFLUENCER MARKETING

- Be coordinated, prepare, budget, and spend time studying and implementing strategy.
- Decide about how you should locate influencers: organically check, subscribe to a network, or function with an agency.
- Be polite and human: people who speak to people and not businesses.

DEVELOP A SCHEDULE

- Will the influencer want to mark monthly/quarterly/half-yearly?
- Include your system of public relations, product launch, etc.

- Give the main executives emails on behalf. Project executive travel schedules and meetings individually.

WHAT INFLUENCER MARKETING IS NOT

Marketing power doesn't just include finding someone with an audience and offering them money or recognition so they can tell you positive things. It's the intent of viral celebrities. Influencers are people who spend time creating and promoting their brands. We should, of course, protect their integrity and the people we have faith in. They are people who are diligent and rely on social media, organic followers after organic followers; people like that are not involved in targeting influencers for money alone.

Marketing influencers are not for fast returns, either. It's the same sort of slow-and-steady strategy as social media, where the marketing doesn't deal directly with the selling of the goods. It's about demonstrating your integrity, reputation, and leadership in your business. What you do, as if people claim that a paper goes to Xerox instead of copying it, or Hoover the floor instead of vacuuming it, is about being synonymous with everything it offers you. It's a slow game to get the kind of followers that are loyal and dedicated to Social Media Marketing. It is tenting to expect that joining forces with an influencer would be an easy path through his followers' hearts and minds, but this is not so straightforward. You must win their confidence and admiration as you associate yourself with influencers. Yet how does this happen?

WHAT DOESN'T WORK IN INFLUENCER MARKETING

Make your approach generalized and use various influencers. Not all influencers have one dimension: customize the approach to the individual influencer.

Look at the influencer's success. Influence is not just notoriety. Note, the goal is to get consumers to take concrete action. Don't automatically assume the factors that influence a niche are the people with the most followers.

ONE SIMPLE RULE: INFLUENCER MARKETING IS MARKETING TO INFLUENCERS

With conventional social network marketing, brands can build an identity on any channel they choose, and they can see who they are brand supporters over time and with an increasing fan base. These are the customers who like and share their content or mention the brand in a post. This is accompanied by personal attention and as part of a highly segmented network of all brand champions. Efforts to promote this category focus on ways to develop it further.

One issue with this strategy is that there are not enough followers of a brand to have a significant impact. Most ordinary people do not do so on social media. Most people have a wide network of several hundred friends and workers representing all sorts of interests and tastes. In the meantime, brands are trying to select and build products they hope will hit their followers substantially, while also participating in regular interactions.

This distributed social media approach produces predictable and unpredictable outcomes. Installer marketing advises us that our time is best spent appealing directly to influencers whose preferences and dislikes we know; they'd write rather than desperately seek to find likes and followers or to throw new content to find out what goes on and our matches. Good plays.

This means engaging these individuals via social media, not only following and caring but also interacting and displaying personality and knowledge. This may also indicate the curating or production of material that is deliberately selected to attract influencers' attention. Although the consumer of the influence is the lowest price, it is influencers themselves who are the target market for marks.

BY LAYING THIS GROUNDWORK, YOU CAN ACHIEVE TWO THINGS AS A BRAND

Firstly, through simple, optimistic, and supportive social contact with influencers, you early gain access to your followers. As a member of your culture, they don't support them and raise their overall reputation. They reveal your face.

The second achievement is that they already know you when you are suggesting some sort of marketing partnership. Fluids are not celebrities per se, but they can live online very much like the person they are known for- they can be disrupted by people they don't know and who would like to compliment or discourage them at the moment they spend time. You must be able to differentiate yourself from the noise of emails and tweets received. This means that they know what it's all about when you turn finally to them, and they know that you're right for their audience.

AN INFLUENCER MARKETING CAMPAIGN: CASE STUDY

The previous case of PewDiePie could have given you an idea of what a marketing strategy might look like in action. However, it may be difficult to see how this kind of approach will impact some of the business world's less attractive areas. Let's take an example in this regard -- The Content Marketing Conference campaign to encourage the conference's participation and awareness. A more conservative approach may have focused only on SEO and Google Advertising, as well as on Twitter and LinkedIn posts. Maybe there would have been a blog post, which is divisible and reveals the word.

Alternatively, the Institute of Content Marketing partnered with Top Rank Marketing to create a multimedia strategy to spread the message. To be honest, there is already a relatively large network of influencers with the Content Marketing Institute. It was as straightforward to recognise future workers as to question who was speaking at their meeting. We did just that and asked for any suggestions or advice from the speakers on content marketing. The input was presented in four separate e-books along with other instructional resources, each with a particular topic of its importance for the CMI conference schedule. - the eBook was available for SlideShare viewing or for downloading as a PDF, which included links distributed by CMI, Top Rank, and influencers via social media. Curata, a software developer specialized in content processing and management platforms, signed the entire initiative.

Many players are in a campaign but look at how everyone works.

- For the conference, the target audience was recruited with free, exciting, and useful personal information. More than 230,000 people saw SlideShare's e-books, while 4,000 downloaded PDFs.
- The platform was used by participating influencers to promote participation in their conference sessions. By sharing e-books, they had more chances to raise awareness and make people more credible and respected in their fields.
- CMI had the presence that they were looking for and had another important conference with them, which they held in the centre of everything.
- Over 1,000 new business opportunities were provided for Curata, who paid for it.

In these campaigns, no promotional tricks were used, no fake celebrities smiled at a product or service they never used. Think it like this; a direct brand marketing game funded by people who wrote the brand commercialization book and targeted others in their campaigns was the CMI conference program. Some are familiar with the "trade tricks," but the plan succeeded. And that's because there's no trick in this scenario.

- The best social marketing works because it's just a natural social relationship.

- The best content marketing works because it is useful information.
- And marketing is the best influence because it is based on content and social marketing tools, in which the public's minds are already rooted in credibility and real authority.

CONCLUSION

The marketing of persuasion uses our knowledge of human psychology to develop techniques for marketing products or services. In this case, this applies especially to the marketing mix advertising aspect and depends on the impulsive behaviour of customers to purchase them.

Concerning web trade, the design of a website is part of persuasion marketing. The application of human psychology to web design in this area, which focusses on the non-consciously controlled decision-making, encourages website visitors to take certain steps and make certain decisions instead of free to choose how they interact with their website with elements such as design, copying, and typography together with the correct advertising messages.

For a long time, sellers have employed convincing techniques and are now working on the Internet to translate these techniques. It is a strategic subject and approach for vendors in a range of industries. You want to transform visits into sales when you have a website for ecommerce and using marketing tactics simplifies this process.

One of the persuasive marketing theories is that consumers are receptive to compelling claims based on a variety of factors, including their immediate emotional state. A seller or distributor will look for a "persuasion window" to increase the chances of attracting a buyer, open one if necessary, and conclude the deal before it closes.

Just imagine a visitor who subscribed to a website newsletter and who has made a page for "thank you." Since this visitor has already looked after this website and is in an "interactive" state, the "thanks" pages generally conversion rates of 39 percent are additional offers.

The "wake up" website is another way to create attractive windows. Many marketers design pages so that people have reasons to regularly review them so that missing opportunities or offers are avoided. When you visit a website in your spare time, you are already persuaded.

COMMUNICATION

Structured communication, like the "planned conversation" of interpersonal sales, involves monitoring the order of dialogue and how the consumer receives information. The aim is to move a customer down his "momentum curve," first promote the momentum of a customer and then call for action after it has reached its highest level. This means, in website design, that the client's first page does not search automatically for the offer but provides the first message and promotes more website exploration.

STORYTELLING

Storytelling uses an emotional and unconscious reaction system to unify or monitor the more objective reactions of a consumer. By using certain words and images that emotional responses are produced, such as love, familiarity, empathy, and a desire to succeed, storytelling is a critical element in marketing.

COPYWRITING

For titles, subtitles, product descriptions, and other texts, copywriting uses compelling words and phrases to attract buyers. If you scan material, and most web pages are scanned before reading, for example, questions stand out rather than statements. "What is the best way to catch attention?" is more attractive than "How to catch the focus." The persuasion supplier is testing different types of copies on the site to determine the emotions or responses which are most likely to produce them.

Different words describing the same thing may connote very differently. For instance, "decisions" produce a positive emotional answer and "commitment" a negative answer. The writer and the seller must also bear in mind that a loss of fear is more motivating than the promise of profit for most people. "Don't miss out," therefore, has more impact than "This may be yours."

PSYCHOLOGY

Neuromarketing is perhaps the critical component of persuasive marketing and psychology applies to the message of marketing. Psychological research reveals information on the diverse factors contributing to a decision, up to 90 percent of which occur outside of our conscious thinking. For example, studies show that in "preparing," a particular mood, visual and olfactory indications are essential. Supermarkets display flowers on the front to "strengthen" the image of freshness to customers. When it comes to website design, colour schemes and other photos are being used to enhance website user responses.

UNDERSTANDING YOUR BUYER

Although buyer comprehension can improve almost anything, buyer research has the most significant effect on sales and marketing. The sales and marketing team process, key activities, organization, metrics, content, communication, and technology can and should be based on an in-depth understanding of the buyer. This approach can make a company capable of achieving its sales goals; this can be simple but powerful.

Since consumer analysis, which helps marketers understand who the consumer is, what they want, and how they decide, may boost a range of measures in the chain of sales. Included in these indicators are higher conversion rates, shorter selling times, and greater average orders.

Although the business impact of buyer research can be substantial, very few companies contribute effectively to buyer comprehension. Most businesses think that gathering customer information is an expensive and time-consuming process that produces low-quality outcomes. This is not the way buyer research needs to be. Marketing and sales can take five simple steps to understand the customer quickly.

Understanding your buyer will give you a perfect vision of marketing to them, what they are, their problems, psychological attachment, and how to get them to buy from you.

About the Author

Ioannis Antypas is a Serial Entrepreneur, Investor, Author and currently the CEO & Founder of the Antypas Group, a Group that consists of multiple companies that create outside-of-the box solutions to common corporate issues.

Prior to funding the Antypas Group, Antypas had a long history and relationship with the importing and exporting industry for over 10 years. His business legacy arose and was seen through his ownership of different restaurants in London. He has supported multiple large-scale businesses which include LF Cars, ANAAM Cars, Milano Stone and more.

His driving forces constantly fall under the umbrella of self-improvement and development, as well as a desire to help businesses and individuals reach their full potential. As a result, he often sponsors different Foundations, especially those who help underprivileged children escape poverty, alongside educational programs focusing on leadership development and the acquisition of business skills.

In order for the world to hold constant progressive elements, the need for qualified leaders quickly becomes of importance. This is something Antypas holds in mind as the search for an improved society becomes evident and being part of the process becomes the only solution.

www.ingramcontent.com/pod-product-compliance
Lightning Source LLC
Chambersburg PA
CBHW060025210326
41520CB00009B/1000